The End of Poverty

Peter Edward · Andy Sumner

The End of Poverty

Inequality and Growth in Global Perspective

Peter Edward
Newcastle University Business School
Newcastle upon Tyne, UK

Andy Sumner
Department of International Development
King's College London
London, UK

ISBN 978-3-030-14763-1   ISBN 978-3-030-14764-8 (eBook)
https://doi.org/10.1007/978-3-030-14764-8

Library of Congress Control Number: 2019932959

© The Editor(s) (if applicable) and The Author(s), under exclusive licence to Springer Nature Switzerland AG 2019

This work is subject to copyright. All rights are solely and exclusively licensed by the Publisher, whether the whole or part of the material is concerned, specifically the rights of translation, reprinting, reuse of illustrations, recitation, broadcasting, reproduction on microfilms or in any other physical way, and transmission or information storage and retrieval, electronic adaptation, computer software, or by similar or dissimilar methodology now known or hereafter developed.

The use of general descriptive names, registered names, trademarks, service marks, etc. in this publication does not imply, even in the absence of a specific statement, that such names are exempt from the relevant protective laws and regulations and therefore free for general use.

The publisher, the authors and the editors are safe to assume that the advice and information in this book are believed to be true and accurate at the date of publication. Neither the publisher nor the authors or the editors give a warranty, expressed or implied, with respect to the material contained herein or for any errors or omissions that may have been made. The publisher remains neutral with regard to jurisdictional claims in published maps and institutional affiliations.

Cover credit: © John Rawsterne/patternhead.com

This Palgrave Pivot imprint is published by the registered company Springer Nature Switzerland AG
The registered company address is: Gewerbestrasse 11, 6330 Cham, Switzerland

Acknowledgements

We would like to thank an anonymous reviewer and those who commented on earlier drafts of this book.

Contents

1	Introduction	1
2	Growth and Distribution Since the Cold War	5
3	A Model of Global Consumption, Output and Distribution	11
4	Global Poverty by Different Poverty Lines Since the Cold War	21
5	The End of Global Poverty	45
6	Conclusion	63
7	Methodological Annex	69
	Index	87

List of Figures

Fig. 3.1	Global density curves, 1990, 2000 and 2012 *without* top income adjustment	17
Fig. 3.2	Global density curves, 1990, 2000 and 2012 *with* top income adjustment	17
Fig. 4.1	Sensitivity of global poverty headcount, 2012, $0–$10 per day	22
Fig. 4.2	Global growth incidence curve, 1990–2012, 1990–2000 and 2000–2012 *without* top income adjustment	32
Fig. 4.3	Global growth incidence curve, excluding China, 1990–2012, 1990–2000 and 2000–2012, *without* top income adjustment	32
Fig. 4.4	Global growth incidence curve, 1990–2012, 1990–2000 and 2000–2012 *with* top income adjustment	33
Fig. 4.5	Absolute change in consumption 1990–2012, *without* top income adjustment	34
Fig. 4.6	Absolute change in consumption, excluding China, 1990–2012, *without* top income adjustment	35
Fig. 4.7	Global poverty headcount (% of global population), 1990–2012	37
Fig. 4.8	Global poverty headcount (% of global population), excluding China, 1990–2012	38
Fig. 4.9	Global poverty headcount (millions), 1990–2012	39
Fig. 4.10	Global poverty headcount (millions), excluding China, 1990–2012	40

Fig. 4.11   Global poverty gap, 1990–2012 (US$bn, 2011 PPP)   41
Fig. 4.12   Global poverty gap, excluding China, 1990–2012
            (US$bn, 2011 PPP)   42

List of Tables

Table 3.1	Coverage of population and HFCE in GrIP v2.0 before and after filling by 2011 and 2005 PPP	13
Table 4.1	Stylised consumption groups based on global consumption, 2012 (2011 PPP$)	26
Table 4.2	Where does each group live and how much do they consume? Data without top income adjustment	30
Table 5.1	Estimates of scale of redistribution of the growth increment, 1990–2012 to eradicate poverty: Data with and without top income adjustment	46
Table 5.2	Estimates of scale of redistribution of the growth increment, 1990–2012 to eradicate $2 poverty, *without* top income adjustment	51
Table 5.3	Estimates of scale of redistribution of the growth increment, 1990–2012 to eradicate $4 poverty, *without* top income adjustment	53
Table 5.4	Estimates of scale of redistribution of the growth increment, 1990–2012 to eradicate $10 poverty, *without* top income adjustment	56
Table 7.1	Conversion multipliers for adjusting income survey data	74
Table 7.2	Estimates of scale of redistribution of the growth increment, 1990–2012 to eradicate $2 poverty, *with* top income adjustment	77

Table 7.3	Estimates of scale of redistribution of the growth increment, 1990–2012 to eradicate $4 poverty, *with* top income adjustment	80
Table 7.4	Estimates of scale of redistribution of the growth increment, 1990–2012 to eradicate $10 poverty, *with* top income adjustment	82

CHAPTER 1

Introduction

Abstract In this introduction we set out the main argument of the book which is as follows: In order to better understand the impact of growth on poverty, it is necessary to consider what happens across a wide range of poverty lines, and to understand how different poverty lines imply very different understandings of how the global economy needs to work if poverty is to be eradicated. This point is not widely recognised because it is not immediately apparent if one focuses only on poverty levels without putting them, as we do, into the context of the distribution of growth across the entire global population.

Keywords Poverty · Inequality · Growth

THE END OF POVERTY

The end of global poverty has long been an aspiration of the UN. Recent progress seems to have brought just that prospect within reach. According to the UN (2015, p. 4), since 1990, global extreme poverty more than halved, falling from 1.9 billion in 1990 to less than 0.9 billion—meeting and surpassing the target set for the Millennium Development Goals (MDGs). This apparent success story was underpinned by dramatic growth in global output and consumption, which have both doubled in the 25 years since the end of the Cold War. These headlines read as a story of the benefits of the spread of global

© The Author(s) 2019
P. Edward and A. Sumner, *The End of Poverty*,
https://doi.org/10.1007/978-3-030-14764-8_1

1

growth since 1990. Today, the end of global poverty is often framed in a narrative that if growth continues, then the world might well meet the Sustainable Development Goals (SDGs) target to 'eradicate extreme poverty for all people everywhere' by 2030.

How fair is such a picture? What progress is being made with poverty reduction? How meaningful is it, and what might be the prospects for further reductions in the future? And, perhaps most importantly of all, if global output has doubled in recent decades, then is the problem one of insufficient growth overall? Just how different would the pattern, or distribution, of global growth need to have been in the period since the end of Cold War in order to have ended poverty already? And what does that history tell us about the likelihood of meeting the UN SDG1 to eradicate extreme poverty by 2030?

These are, of course, contentious issues, as we show in this book. Poverty lines are typically presented as technically based and politically neutral, but in practice, this is far from the case. Different poverty lines carry within them assumptions both about what constitutes the end of global poverty, and about what is implied in terms of the welfare regime required to end poverty in a reasonable time frame. Fortunately, there is a growing set of data about income, consumption and inequality around the world. This data remains far from perfect. That said, it is the data that are used to generate the global poverty headcounts for the SDG target. Thus, it is reasonable to assume that it is good enough to interrogate patterns of growth, and in doing so to address the questions outlined above, if the limitations are not forgotten.

In this book, we describe how we constructed, predominantly from those same data sets used to produce 'official' estimates of global poverty, a model of global consumption that spans the entire global population. We call this the Growth, Inequality and Poverty (GrIP) model. We have previously published work, in a variety of academic papers, using earlier versions of this model (see for example, Edward and Sumner 2013a, b, 2014). That work led us to recognise how narratives of impressive poverty reduction are more fragile than they may first appear. This is largely due to the hypersensitivity of poverty headcounts to small variations in poverty line values. Ten cents on or off a line can equate to 100 million people more or less on the poverty headcount.

Another way of putting this is that a lot of the people who are counted as poor by one poverty line are counted as non-poor by a line barely much higher. When this issue is compounded, in forecasts, with uncertainties (and different assumptions) over future growth rates and trends in inequality distributions, we find that the prospects for eradicating extreme poverty by 2030 are very uncertain (see Edward and Sumner 2014). And even if extreme poverty were to be eradicated by 2030, there would still be a very large number of people living only slightly above the extreme poverty line; a situation that some, maybe many, people would not really consider amounted to the ending of global poverty 'in all its forms' as the SDGs aspire to do.

THE THESIS

The main argument of the book is that to understand better the impact of global growth on poverty, it is necessary to consider what happens across a wide range of poverty lines, and to understand how different poverty lines imply very different understandings of how the global economy needs to work if poverty is to be eradicated. This point is not widely recognised because it is not immediately apparent if one focuses only on poverty levels without putting them, as we do, into the context of the distribution of growth across the entire global population.

The construction of poverty lines is typically presented as a politically neutral, technical matter arising from unbiased statistical analysis of economic data. But, as we show here, different poverty lines lead to very significantly different political implications for how capitalism should be pursued. What seem like impartial statistical decisions not only frame what poverty is thought to be, but they also imply different degrees of challenge to the welfare regime (the set of policies and institutions promoting raised standards of living) and the functioning of the global capitalist economy. The implications of these different challenges typically remain largely unexplored to some considerable extent. We argue that they are hidden by the attention placed instead on the relationship between growth and falling extreme poverty headcounts. As a result, the more complicated and problematic implications of the interrelationship between growth, poverty and the distribution of the benefits of growth are neglected.

Our aim in this book is to bring this omission back in from the cold by exploring this interrelationship. To do this, we ask this question: why has global poverty not been ended yet? Given that the global economy has doubled since the end of the Cold War, we argue that it is not because there has just not been enough growth overall.

So how different would the working of the global economy need to have been to have eradicated poverty by now, and what does that imply for the challenge of the UN SDG1 to eradicate global poverty 'in all its forms' by 2030?

The book is structured as follows: Chapter 2 gives an overview of the issues of contention. In Chapter 3, we outline our methodology and introduce our custom-built global distribution data set (and more detail is provided in the methodological annex). In Chapter 4, we then consider the scale of and trends in global poverty by different poverty lines. In Chapter 5, we ask what it would have taken to end poverty at different poverty lines. Chapter 6 concludes.

References

Edward, P., & Sumner, A. (2013a). *The future of global poverty in a multi-speed world: New estimates of scale and location, 2010–2030* (Center for Global Development Working Paper 327). Washington, DC: CGD.

Edward, P., & Sumner, A. (2013b). *The geography of inequality: Where and by how much has income distribution changed since 1990?* (Centre for Global Development Working Paper 341). Washington, DC: CGD.

Edward, P., & Sumner, A. (2014). Estimating the scale and geography of global poverty now and in the future: How much difference do method and assumptions make? *World Development, 58,* 67–82.

UN. (2015). *The Millennium Development Goals Report.* New York: UN.

CHAPTER 2

Growth and Distribution Since the Cold War

Abstract In this chapter, we lay out the core empirical contention of the book. Specifically, global output and consumption doubled between 1990 and 2012. And yet, despite this dramatic increase in global consumption one in seven people still live on less than $2 a day, and more than one in three people on less than $4 a day (2011 PPP). That is not to say that growth has not been effective. Although growth has been effective at reducing poverty at lower poverty lines, there is a question mark over whether the distribution of growth has been as efficient as it needs to be if the world is to substantially reduce poverty at (slightly) higher, but arguably more reasonable, poverty lines.

Keywords Poverty · Inequality · Growth

Global output and consumption doubled between 1990 and 2012, when measured in purchasing power parity (2005 or 2011 PPP) terms. And yet, despite this dramatic increase in global consumption and in all the attendant environmental and sustainability risks that are implied, one in seven people still live on less than $2 a day, and more than one in three people on less than $4 a day (2011 PPP). That is not to say that growth has not been effective. Growth has certainly been effective in reducing poverty at lower poverty lines, albeit with substantial cross-country variations (see for discussion, Adams 2003; Bourguignon 2003;

Dollar et al. 2013; Edward 2006; Fosu 2011; Kalwij and Verschoor 2007; Kraay 2006; Loayza and Raddatz 2010; Ravallion 1995, 2001, 2005; Ravallion and Chen 1997; White and Anderson 2001).

However, although growth has been effective at reducing poverty at lower poverty lines, there is a question mark over whether the distribution of growth has been as efficient as it needs to be if the world is to substantially reduce poverty at (slightly) higher, but arguably more reasonable, poverty lines.

These issues are particularly relevant because ending global poverty in the near future (defined as being by 2030) has become the focus of much of the discussion around the new UN SDGs. There are numerous poverty projections, almost a small cottage industry, on the plausibility of ending poverty at various lower end poverty lines (e.g. Bluhm et al. 2014; Edward and Sumner 2013, 2014; Dercon and Lea 2012; Hillebrand 2009; Karver et al. 2012; Ravallion 2012, 2013). Such estimates are fragile to assumptions on growth and distribution taken (see for discussion Edward and Sumner 2014) while projections have, to date, been solely based on 'old' or 2005 PPP data, and focus mainly on lower end poverty lines of $1.25 in 2005 PPP, since rebased to $1.90 in 2011 PPP (see Ferreira et al. 2015).

Many, but not all, such projections ignore the interaction of growth with inequality, and instead assume that inequality is static over time on the basis that historically, inequality has risen in as many countries as it has fallen, and overall global within-country inequality has been largely static.

At first sight, recent global success in reducing poverty at lower poverty lines seems to provide strong support for the recent pattern of economic growth as the primary route to eliminate poverty. It deserves reflection that in 1990, the global $2 a day poverty gap (the amount of additional money needed to lift all those living on less than $2 up to that poverty line) was just less than $500bn (at 2011 PPP rates). By 2012, after over $15tr of growth in global consumption (at 2011 PPP rates), that poverty gap was still $200bn. So, while growth might seem to have been an effective way to reduce extreme poverty, there are questions as to whether, due to the distribution of growth, global growth alone can be relied upon to eradicate poverty in the near future. And, since much of the global poverty reduction has occurred in a small number of emerging economies where absolute poverty rates at $2 are now relatively low (notably, China), it can be expected that while these economies will continue to contribute to global growth, the impact of that growth on overall global absolute poverty rates will reduce.

There is a risk that focusing global attention onto poverty defined by very low poverty lines means that the dominant focus is on the effectiveness, rather than the efficiency, of global growth as a route to poverty reduction. Side-stepping issues of efficiency in this way makes it easier to overlook that there may well be limits to global growth, and that the 'easy wins' available in large emerging economies may be less significant in future years. It is necessary, therefore, to go deeper and consider the relationship between growth, inequality and poverty in more detail. To explore this issue of the efficiency of growth as a route to poverty reduction, we investigate how the benefits of global consumption growth have been distributed across various segments of global society. This forms the precursor for going on later to consider how different scenarios of growth redistribution might have led to different degrees of poverty reduction.

Exploring this issue of efficiency requires that, instead of merely investigating the relationship between growth and poverty by focusing solely on what happens to those below the poverty line, one needs also to consider the global distribution of the entire consumption growth increment. Using a custom-built model of consumption, output and distribution, the GrIP model, we start by considering the entire global distribution, from poorest to richest, to identify who has benefited, and by how much, from the doubling of global consumption since 1990. We then explore a range of poverty lines to ask what it would have taken to end global poverty at these various poverty lines. The implication here is that the historical data can inform arguments underpinning the implementation of the UN SDGs on what it would take to end global poverty by 2030.

This leads us to identify that the challenge of eradicating poverty at different poverty lines can have radically different implications. We discuss this by exploring: how much redistribution of the global consumption *growth increment* would have been needed to end poverty; who among the richer peoples of the world might have had to forego some of their increase in consumption to enable this redistribution; and how much that would have impacted on their consumption levels.

Central to our analysis is our acknowledgement that the logic of capitalism is private gain. Therefore, *if* capitalism is to provide a route to the eradication of poverty, a proportion of the global growth increment would, presumably, still need to accrue to the more affluent in order to sustain the incentives for growth. Of course, there is an argument that redistribution of the growth increment could slow aggregate growth. However, Luebker (2007), taking data for 26 countries, found no support for the idea that redistribution impedes future growth. Additionally, other studies have found that redistribution may even be good for growth or at least have a neutral impact on growth (Easterly and Rebelo 1993; Ostry et al. 2014; Perotti 1996).

Recognising, however, that people are unlikely willingly to see a reduction in their existing consumption, but might be somewhat less aggrieved about missing out on part of a potential increase in consumption, we pose the question not as one of the redistribution of consumption (taking from some to give to others), but as one of the distribution of the *growth increment* (regulating the distribution of increases in consumption so that all benefit from growth but more of that growth accrues to the poorest). We therefore ask, under a number of different poverty line scenarios, the question of how much less consumption growth would have accrued to the rich if the world had found a way to direct that growth first to poverty eradication for the poorest (for example, by national growth that raised the consumption of the poorest or by transnational transfers such as foreign aid).

References

Adams, R. (2003). *Economic growth, inequality and poverty: Findings from a new data set* (World Bank Working Paper 2972). Washington, DC: World Bank.

Bluhm, R., De Crombrugghe, D., & Szirmai, A. (2014). *Poor trends: The pace of poverty reduction after the millennium development agenda* (UNU-MERIT Working Paper 2014/006). Maastricht: UNU-MERIT.

Bourguignon, F. (2003). The growth elasticity of poverty reduction: Explaining heterogeneity across countries and time periods. In T. Eicher & S. Turnovsky (Eds.), *Inequality and growth: Theory and policy implications*. Cambridge, MA: MIT Press.

Dercon, S., & Lea, N. (2012). *The prospects of the poor: The future geography of poverty and its implications for DFID*. London: Department for International Development.

Dollar, D., Kleineberg, T., & Kraay, A. (2013). *Growth still is good for the poor* (World Bank Policy Research Working Paper 6568). Washington, DC: World Bank.

Easterly, W., & Rebelo, S. (1993). Fiscal policy and economic growth: An empirical investigation. *Journal of Monetary Economics, 32*(3), 417–458.

Edward, P. (2006). Examining inequality: Who really benefits from global growth? *World Development, 34*(10), 1667–1695.

Edward, P., & Sumner, A. (2013). *The future of global poverty in a multi-speed world: New estimates of scale and location, 2010–2030* (Center for Global Development Working Paper 327). Washington, DC: CGD.

Edward, P., & Sumner, A. (2014). Estimating the scale and geography of global poverty now and in the future: How much difference do method and assumptions make? *World Development, 58*, 67–82.

Ferreira, F., Chen, S., Dabalen, A. L., et al. (2015). *A global count of the extreme poor in 2012: Data issues, methodology, and initial results* (World Bank Working Paper). Washington, DC: World Bank.

Fosu, A. (2011). *Growth, inequality, and poverty reduction in developing countries: Recent global evidence* (World Institute for Development Economics Research Working Paper 2011/01). Helsinki: WIDER.

Hillebrand, E. (2009). *Poverty, growth and inequality over the next 50 years.* Expert meeting on how to feed the world in 2050. Rome: FAO.

Kalwij, A., & Verschoor, A. (2007). Not by growth alone: The role of the distribution of income in regional diversity in poverty reduction. *European Economic Review, 51*(4), 805–829.

Karver, J., Kenny, C., & Sumner, A. (2012). *MDGs 2.0: What goals, targets, and timeframe?* (Center for Global Development Working Paper 297). Washington, DC: CGD.

Kraay, A. (2006). When is growth pro-poor? Evidence from a panel of countries. *Journal of Development Economics, 80*(1), 198–227.

Loayza, N., & Raddatz, C. (2010). The composition of growth matters for poverty alleviation. *Journal of Development Economics, 93*(1), 137–151.

Luebker, M. (2007). Income inequality, inequality and the demand for redistribution: Are the assumptions of the new growth theory valid? *Socio-Economic Review, 5*(1), 117–148.

Ostry, J., Berg, A., & Tsangarides, C. (2014). *Redistribution, inequality, and growth* (International Monetary Fund Staff Discussion Note 14/02). Washington, DC: IMF.

Perotti, R. (1996). Growth, income distribution and democracy: What the data say. *Journal of Economic Growth, 1*(2), 149–187.

Ravallion, M. (1995). Growth and poverty: Evidence for developing countries in the 1980s. *Economic Letters, 48*(3–4), 411–417.

Ravallion, M. (2001). Growth, inequality and poverty: Looking behind the averages. *World Development, 29*(11), 1803–1815.

Ravallion, M. (2005). *Inequality is bad for the poor* (World Bank Policy Research Working Paper 3677). Washington, DC: World Bank.

Ravallion, M. (2012). *Benchmarking global poverty reduction* (Policy Research Working Paper 6205). Washington, DC: World Bank.

Ravallion, M. (2013). *How long will it take to lift one billion people out of poverty?* (World Bank Policy Research Working Paper 6325). Washington, DC: World Bank.

Ravallion, M., & Chen, S. (1997). What can new survey data tell us about recent changes in distribution and poverty? *World Bank Economic Review, 11*(2), 357–382.

White, H., & Anderson, E. (2001). Growth versus distribution: Does the pattern of growth matter? *Development Policy Review, 19*(3), 267–289.

CHAPTER 3

A Model of Global Consumption, Output and Distribution

Abstract In this chapter, we discuss our methodology. We discuss the GrIP model and its construction. This is a custom-built model of global consumption, output and distribution. We focus on the three main construction issues: the data sets used; the global population and consumption coverage; and a new adjustment for this book related to top incomes.

Keywords Poverty · Inequality · Growth

In this chapter, we discuss our methodology (see also the extended discussion in the methodological annex). The estimates provided in the later chapters of this book are based on the GrIP model. This is a custom-built model of global consumption, output and distribution discussed and originally developed by Edward (2006), and further discussed (and updated and expanded) in Edward and Sumner (2014, 2015a, b, 2016). Here we focus on the three main construction issues: the data sets used; the global population and consumption coverage; and a new adjustment for this book related to top incomes.

GrIP is a global model of consumption and distribution built of data drawn from several data sets, with adjustments made for consistency. The principal data sets are: the World Bank's *PovcalNet*; *World Development Indicators* (henceforth, WDI); and the United Nations' World Institute of Development Economics (UNU-WIDER), *World Income Inequality Database* (henceforth, WIID).

Throughout this book, we use the 2011 PPP rates, released in 2014, that updated and superseded earlier 2005 PPP rates. Our reasons for this are that, notwithstanding various methodological critiques, the 2011 PPP rates are generally considered to be more reliable than the 2005 rates because of improvements in methodology (Deaton and Aten 2014). Furthermore, because they lead to lower poverty estimates for a given poverty line, using the 2011 rates generates a more favourable perspective on the impact of global growth on poverty reduction (thus ensuring that any conclusions are conservative with regard to the difficulties inherent in eradicating poverty).

In this book, we have chosen not to take the analysis further back than 1990. Pragmatically, this is because the 2011 PPP figures (in WDI) have been backdated, but only to 1990. We could have extended this backdating, but it becomes less reliable the further one extrapolates it. Also, the coverage of national household income and consumption distribution surveys gets a lot less complete once one goes back to the 1980s or earlier. We therefore provide analysis here only from 1990, a starting point that does, however, neatly cover a period in history, namely the period of contemporary globalisation that has played a role in shaping global economic growth since the end of the Cold War.

The core approach in the GrIP model is to take for each country the survey distribution data and, by combining this with data on national population and on the mean consumption per capita in internationally comparable PPP $, and develop for each country an estimate of how many people live at any specific consumption level ($-a-day 2011 PPP). Having identified for each country the number of people living at a given consumption level, GrIP then aggregates these to build a global distribution. A wide variety of other aggregations are also readily produced; for example, by region or income category. These aggregations can then be interrogated to investigate issues such as poverty levels and trends in inequality, and the distribution of the benefits of economic growth. A number of methodological issues arise in making the best use of the available data to build a global model of consumption distribution, and these are discussed next.

GrIP predominantly uses survey distributions from Povcal. These are drawn from national surveys, usually household surveys, of consumption or income distribution. The Povcal distributions are supplemented where

Table 3.1 Coverage of population and HFCE in GrIP v2.0 before and after filling by 2011 and 2005 PPP

	2011 PPP			2005 PPP		
	No. of countries	Population	HFCE	No. of countries	Population	HFCE
PovcalNet coverage						
1990	110	88.1	82.5	110	88.1	81.1
2012	111	86.9	77.3	109	85.8	73.4
Process 1: additional distributions from WDI and WIID						
1990	130	94.0	97.3	128	93.8	96.9
2012	145	94.6	96.5	143	93.5	94.6
Process 2: filling with estimates for countries with no survey data						
1990	175	96.8	100.6	169	96.4	99.0
2012	192	98.1	100.8	180	96.5	98.0

Note Process 2 figures for HFCE coverage exceed 100% because the WDI 2011 PPP figure for global total HFCE is actually slightly lower than the sum of the HFCE figures for the individual countries.
Source GrIP v2.0

possible with additional distribution data drawn (in order of preference) from WDI or WIID (Process 1 in Table 3.1). Surveys can be based on consumption or income distribution. In the past, analysts have tended to ignore the difference, but recent work by Lahoti et al. (2014) has suggested a useful way to adjust income surveys to align with consumption surveys, and that adjustment is included in the analysis in this book. Surveys do not take place annually, so in the GrIP model, distributions for intermediate years between surveys are calculated by interpolation, while in years subsequent to the most recent survey, or prior to the earliest survey, the distribution is assumed to remain unchanged from that survey (see Dang et al. [2014] for discussion of such issues).

Often, several years can elapse between national distribution surveys. In view of this, and because extrapolation is less reliable than interpolation, in this analysis we limit the most recent year of analysis to 2012 in order to reduce the number of cases where, in the absence of a post-2012 survey, we need to resort to extrapolation. Where a country has no usable surveys, or the gaps between surveys are too great to allow reliable interpolation, we programme the GrIP model to 'fill' a country's missing distributions with a distribution estimated from other similar countries (Process 2 in Table 3.1). The extent of coverage of the GrIP analysis, and the impact of the various process stages in extending this coverage is summarised in Table 3.1, and illustrates the extent to which GrIP represents a global model of consumption distribution incorporating almost all of the global population.

It has long been recognised that the consumption (or income) means (consumption per person per annum, for example) identified in surveys do not reveal a consistent systematic relationship (both between countries and even across time within a single country) with national account (NA) means (HFCE[1] per capita). Comparisons of the impact of using the different means (survey or NA) were first made in the early to mid-2000s by Deaton (2005), Ravallion (2003) and Sala-i-Martin (2002). More recently, Edward and Sumner (2014) used GrIP v1.0 with 2005 PPP data to highlight the importance of adjusting poverty lines to take account of systemic differences between survey and NA data, and to demonstrate how these different approaches lead to substantially differing views on the geography (meaning location) and scale of global poverty.

In this book, we only use the survey-based approach because this mirrors the approach used for PovcalNet and in World Bank poverty estimates. We do this as follows: for every survey in PovcalNet, GrIP calculates the ratio between the NA mean and the survey mean (the NA/S ratio). For years between surveys, NA/S ratios are estimated by interpolation, and for years beyond the range of available surveys the closest relevant NA/S ratio is used (i.e. similar to the approach used for survey distributions). For countries added or filled (Process 1 and Process 2 countries), no survey mean data are available, so the NA/S ratio is estimated from the country's HFCE per capita value using a relationship derived from all the available PovcalNet data. NA/S ratios are then combined with relevant HFCE data from WDI so that the consumption mean applied in GrIP for any given country–year combination makes the best use of all the relevant data available in PovcalNet and WDI.

Once the country distribution (data on quintile and top and bottom decile shares are used) and consumption means are identified, they have to be combined to determine the consumption distribution (the number of people living at each consumption level) for that country. In earlier versions of GrIP, a linear distribution algorithm (described in Edward 2006) was used that accurately replicates the consumption level in each

---

[1] HFCE—Household Final Consumption Expenditure.

fractile in the source data. This works well in the lower fractiles where poverty headcounts are estimated, but at the higher end of the distribution (typically the upper quintile: the highest consuming 20%), while it does accurately reproduce the totals of these top two deciles, it does so at the expense of significant oversimplification of the large variations in inequality within those deciles.

In GrIP v2.0, a facility was added to use the generalised quadratic (GQ) function, as described by Datt (1998). This replicates better the inequality within these highest deciles (in almost all cases, it is the GQ function that gives the best fit). In this book, we use the linear estimation method for poverty lines up to and including $4. However, when looking at higher cut-offs and when considering the global distribution across all consumption levels, we consider that the GQ function is likely to be more representative of the distribution within the highest quintiles. Therefore, when looking at the cut-offs and population segments above $4 and when presenting analysis that covers the full range of global consumption, the analysis is derived from the GQ Lorenz function.

A new feature of the GrIP model, introduced for this book, is an adjustment for top incomes. It is widely recognised that the share of the distribution that accrues to the top percentiles can be substantial, judging by data from the Paris School of Economics' *Top Incomes Project* (TIP) which is based on taxation data (see Alvaredo et al. 2014). It is also recognised that the top of the distribution is not well captured in the household survey data (see for discussion, Korinek et al. 2006). Various methods have been proposed recently to take account of this. Some scholars have attempted to adjust for 'top incomes' by assuming that discrepancies between survey and NA data are entirely due to underreporting by the richest (e.g. Lakner and Milanovic 2013). Others develop assumptions on the missing 'top incomes' using different methods but the same data set (e.g. Anand and Segal 2015). If one is simply making poverty estimates at low poverty lines, then the problem of 'missing' consumption of the richest in society is largely incidental and could be ignored because it occurs at the top of the country distributions, and so generally well above the poverty lines under consideration. However, the issue could make a difference when considering global consumption redistribution, as we do here, because it raises the possibility that the size and difficulty of the global challenge of removing poverty, at the different poverty cut-offs we consider, might be different if one takes into account the missing top incomes.

In GrIP v2.0, we use the Paris TIP data set to develop a relationship between the share of the top decile (10%) in PovcalNet surveys, and the reported shares in TIP of the top 10%, top 5% and top 1%. We use the most recent surveys from each country in TIP where there is both a matching income-based survey in PovcalNet and data in TIP for the top 10%, top 5% and top 1%. This yields 17 datapoints (all of which are from high-income countries [HICs]) from which we derive linear relationships to estimate, from the unadjusted top decile share in the survey distributions in GrIP, revised shares of the top 10, 5 and 1% in each country.[2] The data in GrIP is then adjusted by adding consumption appropriately to the top 10% in each country to bring the shares of these top fractiles in line with these estimated revised shares. Recognising, however, that the NA HFCE figure probably provides an upper limit to the amount of consumption that should reasonably be allocated to any country, we cap the adjustment so that the total consumption for each country does not exceed its NA HFCE total.[3]

This adjustment does not have any impact on the absolute consumption of those below the top decile in each country. It simply adds consumption to the top 10% in each country and distributes this so as to reproduce, in GrIP's consumption-based analysis, the same share of the distribution that the TIP database identifies for and among the top 10%. In practice, however, the share of the rich in a consumption survey will probably be lower than this, as the taxation data used for TIP measures income. GrIP, as configured for the analysis in this book, is being used as a model of consumption rather than income. But rich people tend not to consume as high a proportion of their annual income as do poor people, diverting more income instead to savings and investments. We therefore consider that this top income adjustment in GrIP most probably overstates the share of consumption that is accounted for by the richest decile in each country. Thus, we suggest that our analyses with top income

---

[2] The countries and years used in the analysis are: Australia 2003, Canada 2010, Denmark 2010, Finland 2007, France 2005, Germany 2007, Ireland 2007, Italy 2008, Japan 2008, Netherlands 2010, Norway 2010, Spain 2010, Sweden 2005, Switzerland 2004, United Kingdom 2010, United States 2010, Uruguay 2012. One eligible country (Malaysia 2009) was omitted because the PovcalNet share to the top 10% is actually higher than that shown in TIP.

[3] There are some exceptions to this where the PovcalNet survey mean already implies a consumption level higher than the HFCE total. In those cases, we reason that the HFCE figures must be questionable and so do not apply the cap.

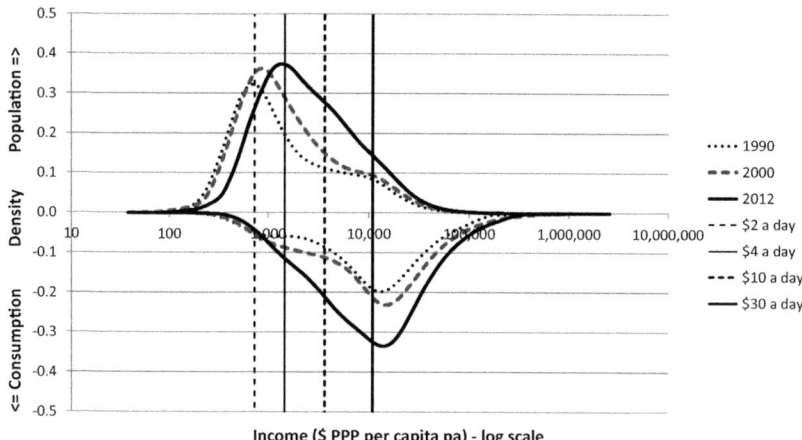

Fig. 3.1 Global density curves, 1990, 2000 and 2012 *without* top income adjustment (*Source* GrIP v2.0)

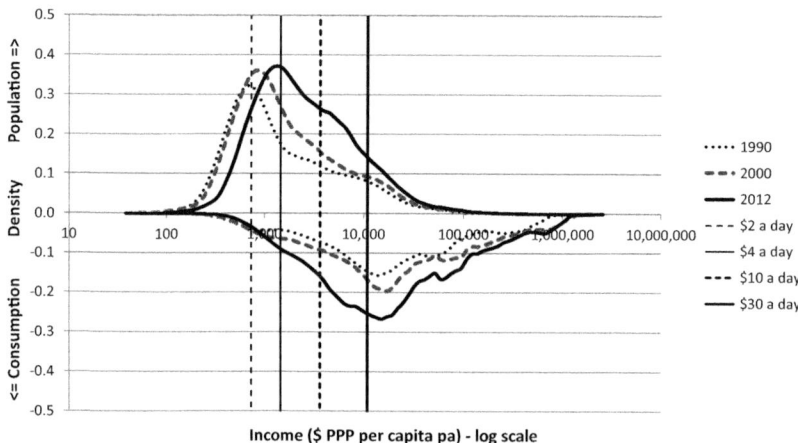

Fig. 3.2 Global density curves, 1990, 2000 and 2012 *with* top income adjustment (*Source* GrIP v2.0)

adjustment (Fig. 3.1) and without top income adjustment (Fig. 3.2) might be seen as bracketing a 'high end' and 'low end' scenario. In the text below, we refer to estimates without top income adjustment unless explicitly stated.

Figures 3.1 and 3.2 present global density curves that illustrate the distribution of population (plotted positively on the y-axis) and consumption (plotted negatively on the y-axis) across the full range of global consumption. Areas beneath curves (that is, between each curve and the x-axis) are standardised relative to the 2012 population and consumption totals, respectively. This means that the differences in these areas between 1990 and 2012 (say) are proportional to the change in the number of people living at any particular consumption level (above the x-axis) or to the change in aggregate consumption of the people living at a particular consumption level (below the x-axis). Figure 3.1 presents the figures without the top incomes adjustment. Figure 3.2 includes the top incomes adjustment.

What can be clearly seen is the growth in the global middle, evidenced by the filling out of the concavity in the population curve (notably around the region of the $4 and $10 a day lines) since 1990. This concavity, which was even deeper in the 1980s, led Quah (1996) to describe us as living in a 'twin-peak' world. It remains to be seen, however, whether the current situation represents a permanent end to that twin-peak rich–poor divide or whether it indicates merely a transition to the emergence of a new divide. For example, the incipient return of the concavity between $4 and $10 a day when top incomes are added in might be a precursor of the return of such a divide. It is notable also that when China is removed, the concavity persists still in 2012, indicating that its current absence at the global level may merely be evidence of China's progressive transition from the lower under-developed peak to a higher-developed location, rather than an indicator of any more fundamental changes in the fairness of the rest of the global economy.

The curves also clearly illustrate who benefited most from global consumption growth. Between 1990 and 2012, global consumption (as measured here using the adjustment in GrIP described above to align NA figures to household survey data) increased by 90%, with most of that growth occurring after 2000; reminding us that despite the financial crisis of the late 2000s, the world is still consuming a lot more now than it was at the end of the Cold War. Of that growth, four-fifths went to those who in 2012 were consuming more than $10 a day. The remaining one fifth (the figure falls to 15% if top incomes are included) went to the more than two-thirds of the world's population who exist more or less precariously on less than $10 a day.

REFERENCES

Alvaredo, F., Atkinson, A., Piketty, T., & Saez, E. (2014). *The world top incomes database*. http://wid.world.

Anand, S., & Segal, P. (2015). The global distribution of income. In Anthony B. Atkinson & François Bourguignon (Eds.), *Handbook of income distribution* (Vol. 2). Amsterdam: Elsevier.

Dang, H.-A., Lanjouw, P., & Serajuddin, U. (2014). *Updating poverty estimates at frequent intervals in the absence of consumption data: Methods and illustration with reference to a middle-income country* (World Bank Policy Research Working Paper 7043). Washington, DC: World Bank.

Datt, G. (1998). *Computational tools for poverty measurement and analysis* (FCND Discussion Papers). Washington, DC: International Food Policy Research Institute (IFPRI).

Deaton, A. (2005). Measuring poverty in a growing world (or measuring growth in a poor world). *The Review of Economics and Statistics, 87*(1), 1–19.

Deaton, A., & Aten, B. (2014). *Trying to understand the PPPs in ICP2011: Why are the results so different?* (National Bureau of Economic Research Working Paper 20244). Cambridge, MA: NBER.

Edward, P. (2006). Examining inequality: Who really benefits from global growth? *World Development, 34*(10), 1667–1695.

Edward, P., & Sumner, A. (2014). Estimating the scale and geography of global poverty now and in the future: How much difference do method and assumptions make? *World Development, 58*, 67–82.

Edward, P., & Sumner, A. (2015a). *New estimates of global poverty and inequality: How much difference do price data really make?* (Center for Global Development Working Paper 403). Washington, DC: CGD.

Edward, P., & Sumner, A. (2015b). Philanthropy, welfare capitalism or radically different global economic model: What would it take to end global poverty within a generation based on historical growth patterns? (Center for Global Development [CGD] Working Paper). Washington DC: CGD.

Edward, P., & Sumner, A. (2016). *Global inequality and global poverty since the cold war?* (CROP Working Paper). Bergen: CROP/UiB.

Korinek, A., Mistiaen, J., & Ravallion, M. (2006). Survey nonresponse and the distribution of income. *Journal of Economic Inequality, 4*(2), 33–55.

Lahoti, R., Jayadev, A., & Reddy, S. (2014). *The global consumption and income project (GCIP): An introduction and preliminary findings*. www.globalconsumptionandincomeproject.org. Accessed 4 June 2018.

Lakner, C., & Milanovic, B. (2013). *Global income distribution: From the fall of the Berlin wall to the great recession* (World Bank Policy Research Working Paper 6719). Washington, DC: World Bank.

Quah, D. (1996). Twin peaks: Growth and convergence in models of distribution dynamics. *The Economic Journal, 106*(437), 1045–1055.

Ravallion, M. (2003). Measuring aggregate welfare in developing countries: How well do national accounts and surveys agree? *The Review of Economics and Statistics, 85*(3), 645–652.

Sala-i-Martin, X. (2002). *The world distribution of income (estimated from individual country distributions)*. Mimeo. New York, NY: Columbia University.

CHAPTER 4

Global Poverty by Different Poverty Lines Since the Cold War

Abstract In this chapter, we discuss trends in global poverty since the Cold War taking several poverty lines. We provide a basis for a set of stylised consumption groups based on global consumption and show how the benefits of growth were distributed since 1990.

Keywords Poverty · Inequality · Growth

It was much heralded in the run-up to the 2015 end-date for the MDGs that substantial progress had been made in reducing global extreme poverty. The GrIP analysis confirms that this is indeed the case, with headcounts below the new $1.90-a-day extreme poverty line falling by more than half, from 1.8bn in 1990 to 0.9mn in 2012. Yet again, though, the rapid rise of China has been a dominant effect. In the rest of the world, extreme poverty fell by just 28%, from 1.1bn to 0.8mn, meaning that over 90% of global extreme poverty is now outside China.

Recalling that the $1.90 poverty line is measured in purchasing power parity (PPP) dollars, it is worth observing that this represents a level of consumption that is 'extreme' poverty and is labelled as such. This means that it is *not* absolute poverty but something below (perhaps destitution). For most people living at this level, the difference between living just 10 cents below or 10 cents above the poverty line could hardly be considered to represent a substantively different quality of life.

© The Author(s) 2019
P. Edward and A. Sumner, *The End of Poverty*,
https://doi.org/10.1007/978-3-030-14764-8_4

Nevertheless, it is by crossing this threshold that people are no longer deemed to be in extreme poverty by the World Bank.

Indeed, poverty headcounts are hypersensitive. Figure 4.1 demonstrates just how sensitive global poverty headcounts are to the choice of poverty line. The $1.90-a-day line is set at a level where the greatest density of the world's population live. In this region, a difference of just 10 cents in the poverty line can add or subtract almost 100mn people to global poverty headcounts. With poverty lines in this region, very modest changes in the poverty line, or in the survey and consumption data on which analyses of poverty headcounts are built, can make very substantial differences to calculated poverty headcounts. It is only when poverty lines increase to around $4–$5 that this sensitivity to measurement and assumption differences starts to reduce significantly.

This is not merely an intriguing statistical issue. The poverty line one adopts makes a substantial difference, not only to the level and trend of global poverty observed, but also influences understandings

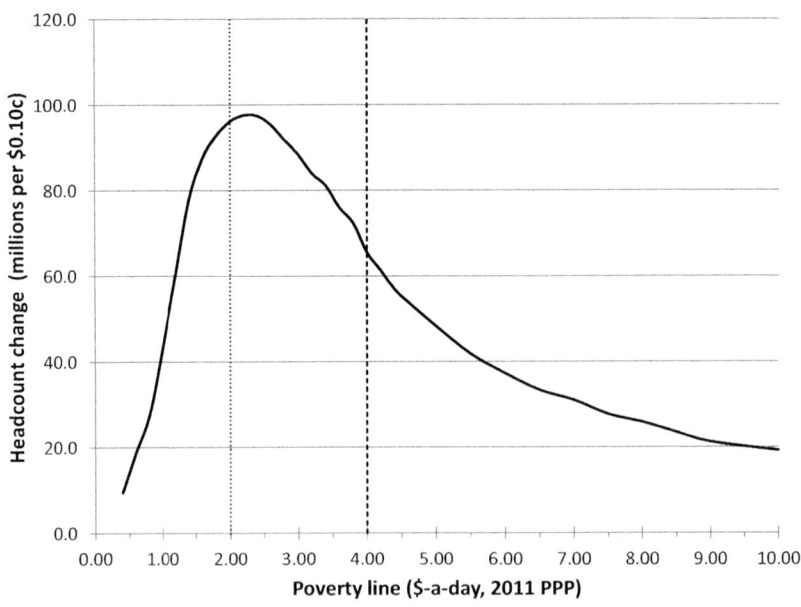

Fig. 4.1 Sensitivity of global poverty headcount, 2012, $0–$10 per day (*Source* GrIP v2.0)

and accompanying narratives of both where the world's 'deserving' poor actually live and the scale of the challenge (in terms of the value of the poverty gap) of ending poverty. Edward and Sumner (2015, 2016) discuss these matters originally raised in Deaton (2010), in more depth. In short, lower poverty lines 'push' global poverty into sub-Saharan Africa and slightly higher lines 'Asianise' global poverty.

What then would be a reasonable global poverty line? The 'official' global poverty line has recently been rebased to $1.90 in 2011 PPP from $1.25 in 2005 PPP (Ferreira et al. 2015; Jolliffe and Prydz 2015). While the logic of this is open to discussion, as in previous adjustments (see Lahoti et al. 2014 and the historic debate between, Ravallion 2002, 2008; Reddy and Pogge 2002, 2005), the new line does have one underlying rationale in that it is the median value in $PPP (2011 PPP) terms of the national poverty lines in the world's low-income countries (LICs) (rather than merely the 15 countries that were used to estimate the earlier $1.25 line). There is though still an arbitrary element here, because the group of LICs is still arbitrary to some extent, although not totally without logic (see Sumner 2016 for discussion).

Jolliffe and Prydz (2015) provide an interesting discussion of the critiques of the international poverty line and propose a new data set of estimates for national poverty lines in 2011 PPP by inferring national poverty lines from the poverty rate to estimate national poverty lines in PPP$. They note (p. 4) that the average poverty line produced—the $1.90 poverty line—from the set of 15 national poverty lines of the poorest countries is very sensitive to quality of inflation data. Mali, for example, requires 22 years of consumer price index (CPI) data to estimate its poverty line in 2011 and in three of the 15 countries (Ghana, Malawi and Tajikistan), the CPI data was thought to be so questionable that household survey data was used to construct a temporal deflator. If CPI in World Development Indicators had been used for those three countries, it would have added 20 cents to the international poverty line and 200mn poor to global poverty counts.

Instead of focusing predominantly on poverty numbers at just the $1.90 poverty line, it is possible to consider poverty numbers across a range of lines (as also proposed by Jolliffe and Prydz 2015). The World Bank has always had two poverty lines, although the higher line ($2 in 2005 PPP) was typically little used. The World Bank has now adopted several lines in principle (see Ferreira et al. 2017). In this book, we adopt this approach by identifying a range of cut-off points at absolute consumption levels across the global consumption distribution. The World Bank takes the median $PPP (2011) values for poverty lines in low-income, lower-middle, upper-middle and high-income countries respectively. We in contrast to the new World Bank approach consider a range of potential global poverty lines, but provide different reference points and draw considerable attention to all lines, not just the lowest.

Our aim is to extend attention away from the very low $1.90 extreme poverty line, and to explore the intermediate terrain occupied by those who may consume more than $1.90 a day but who are still nevertheless very poor. For example, one recent study that estimated different national poverty lines from analysis of food, non-food and housing costs proposed that poverty lines in the region of $2–$4 a day (depending on which country one lives in) were more appropriate for a 'basic needs' poverty line (Allen 2017, p. 3713).

And a different body of empirical studies, that has emerged in response to the growing data on middle-income groups in developing countries, has variously proposed segmentation into different categories of poverty and affluence by reference to daily absolute expenditure per capita ($PPP) with suggested cut-offs between categories ranging from $2/day to $100/day in 2005 PPP (see, for example, Banerjee and Duflo 2008; Birdsall et al. 2014; Easterly 2001; Kharas 2010; Ravallion 2010).

The precedent for segmentation by consumption level lies not in social class theory (which cannot be conflated with consumption data as class is a social identity) but with preference similarity theory—the idea that people with similar purchasing power levels tend, wherever they are in the world, to have broadly similar consumption preferences (Linder 1961). Imagine a group of people spread around the world but all with broadly similar income per capita in PPP terms (i.e. similar spending or consumption power), then we might think of that as a distinct global group or 'segment'.

If one wishes to outline such global groups or segments, so as to demarcate them into global consumption groups, then there are various global reference points that one might look at. One could, for example, consider a person's position relative to:

i. The global distribution peaks for population and consumption (HFCE per capita);

ii. Median HFCE per capita in the industrial/advanced/'rich' world (which we define as OECD HICs) and median HFCE per capita in the developing world (meaning LICs and MICs);
iii. Global consumption fractiles.

By considering these reference points, we estimate, for 2012, a set of stylised global groups or global consumption 'segments'. Of course, the cut-offs between these segments are not really points of 'hard' differentiation: there is not going to be much difference between someone just above or just below the cut-off. But the cut-off points between these stylised groups do nevertheless have globally applicable rationales that justify their relevance for making delineations, in consumption per capita in 2011 PPP$, between these global segments. The groups we identify are: the destitute; the absolute poor; the 'precariat'; the 'securiat'; and the 'prosperiat'. We use the cut-offs of $2 for destitution, $4 for absolute poverty, $10 for security from poverty (thus the precariat is $4–$10) and $30 per day and above for prosperity. Table 4.1 shows the groups and the logic of the differentiation of segments.

The justification for the cut-offs is as follows. The global destitute are those who live on below $2 per day. This population is very poor even by developing country standards as it is below half of the median consumption for all developing countries (which was $4.3 in 2012). It is also approximately the median of the national poverty line of all LICs (see Jolliffe and Prydz 2015). This level of expenditure cut-off includes all the population in the world's poorest decile and 40% of the next decile above the poorest. Table 4.1 shows where this and each segment live and their consumption. This destitute segment amounts to almost a billion people, one in ten of whom live in China. Three in ten live in India and a further four in ten live in sub-Saharan Africa. A third live in low-income or least developed countries and the remainder live in MICs.

The global absolute poor are those who live on below $4 a day (note that we define the 'absolute poor' as a segment that includes all those living below $4 a day, so the 'destitute' are included in and are a subset of the 'absolute poor'). This population is poor by developing country standards. This population live at or below the mode (peak) of the global population curve (which is $3.7) and below the median consumption per capita for developing countries ($4.3). The mean of these reference points is $4 which we take as the cut-off, so that this segment broadly equates to the world's poorest 40% globally. This group amounts

Table 4.1 Stylised consumption groups based on global consumption, 2012 (2011 PPP$)

	Destitute	Absolute poor	Precariat	Securiat	Prosperiat
	Very poor by developing country standards	Poor by developing country standards	Not poor by developing country standards but poor by OECD HIC standards	Not poor by OECD HIC standards but below the OECD HIC median	Above OECD HIC median
Daily consumption per capita (2011 PPP$)	0–2	0–4	4–10	10–30	30+
Global position with reference to global consumption and population curves from GrIP	Below 50% of the median consumption for developing countries ($4.3)	At or below peak of global population curve (less than $3.7) Below median for developing countries ($4.3)	Above peak of global population curve ($3.7) At or above median for developing countries ($4.3) At or below poorest decile upper limit in OECD HICs ($9.5)	Above the poorest decile in OECD HICs ($9.5) At or below the OECD HIC median ($27.8) At or below the median ($27.3) of the global consumption distribution curve Below the mode ($35+) of the global consumption distribution curve	Above the OECD HIC median ($27.8) Above the median ($27.3) of the global consumption distribution curve At or above the mode ($35+) of the global consumption distribution curve

(continued)

Table 4.1 (continued)

	Destitute	Absolute poor	Precariat	Securiat	Prosperiat
Global position with reference to poverty lines	Median poverty line of LICs = $1.92 (see Jolliffe and Prydz 2015)	Median poverty line of developing countries = $3.08 (see Jolliffe and Prydz 2015)	Below 'security from poverty' line of $10 (see López-Calva and Ortiz-Juarez 2014)	Above 'security from poverty' line of $10 (see López-Calva and Ortiz-Juarez 2014)	Substantially above the 'security from poverty' line of $10 (see López-Calva and Ortiz-Juarez 2014)
Global position relative to global consumption deciles	Decile 1, plus 40% of decile 2 ($0–2)	Decile 1–4 ($0–$4.2)	Decile 5–7 ($4.2–$10.8)	Decile 8–9 ($10.8–$29.3)	Decile 10 ($29.3+)

Source Authors' elaboration based on estimates from GrIP v2.0 (without top income adjustment)

to 2.7bn people. About one third (900m) of this segment live in India, 670m in sub-Saharan Africa and 360m in China. Most (2 billion) live in MICs and about 600–650m live in low-income or least developed countries.

Third, the 'precariat' (or insecure by global standards—drawing on Standing 2011; López-Calva and Ortiz-Juarez 2014) are those who are not the absolute poor by developing country standards but are both at risk of sliding back into poverty and are poor by rich/industrial country (OECD HIC) standards. These people consume above the mode (peak) of the global population curve and above the developing country median. However, the precariat consume at or below the upper limit of the poorest decile in rich/advanced countries ($9.5) and constitute the global deciles 5–7 (the upper limit of which is $10.8). So, while they are in the middle in global terms—within this group is the global median ($5.5)—they are poor in rich country terms. Importantly, the $10 per day level is an approximation of a 'security from poverty' line.[1] Those living in this group are approximately 2 billion in number. Of the group, 600m live in China, 250m elsewhere in East Asia and 300m in India. Just 170m live in sub-Saharan Africa. The overwhelming majority live in MICs. Just 100–130m of the 2 billion live in low-income or least developed countries.

Next, we identify a secure 'middle' or 'securiat' consuming between $10 and $30 per day. This includes those people who are not poor by OECD HIC standards and who live above the $10 'security from poverty' line (noted above) but who are still at or below the OECD HIC median ($27.8). They live above the poorest decile in rich/advanced countries (OECD HIC) so could 'afford' to live in rich/advanced countries, although some two-thirds of them live in developing countries. The $30 upper cut-off for this group is also relevant in terms of the global consumption curve. It is both slightly above the median of the global

---

[1] The $10 poverty line is a proposal for a 'security from poverty' consumption line developed and used by López-Calva and Ortiz-Juarez (2014) based on the 10% probability of falling back below national poverty lines (which are $4–$5/day in 2005 PPP) in the near future in Mexico, Brazil and Chile. The 10% probability line is actually $8.50–$9.70 depending on whether Brazil, Mexico or Chile are used (and comparable estimates for Indonesia are $8.37 for a $4 national poverty line and $13.03 at $5, in 2005 PPP—see Sumner et al. 2014). Thus, the mean is $9.27 and if the mean is inflated to 2011 prices it is $10.47. However, given that this is not intended to be a precise estimate—rather, a rough proxy used for illustration purposes here—$10 per capita is used here in 2011 PPP.

consumption curve, or the point at which there is equal consumption above and below this consumption level ($27.3, which occurs at the 89th percentile of the global population) and a little below the mode/peak of the global consumption curve (which throughout the period from 1990 to 2012 has been in the region of $35 to $40). The population in this group broadly equate to global consumption deciles 8 and 9 (decile 9 has an upper limit of $29.3). Those living in this group total 1.5bn in number, of which 1 billion live in developing countries and almost exclusively in MICs. China accounts for 370m of that 1 billion. Other countries in East Asia account for another 200m. Latin America accounts for 180m and the Middle East and North Africa region for 140m.

Finally, there is a prosperous group or 'prosperiat' who consume above $30 per day. This group lives above the OECD HIC median and above the mode of the global consumption curve ($27.3). This segment amounts to just 700m people, of which 130m live in developing countries and 500m live in OECD HICs mostly in Europe and North America. Effectively forming just the richest 10% of the world's population, this group accounts for almost half of global consumption. To put this into context, this group is by no means merely those who are considered rich by developed country standards as it includes 46% of the population of the OECD HICs—in other words, most of this group comprises people who would be considered comfortably in the 'middle' but not rich in the developed world.

Using these proposed cut-offs, in Table 4.2 we summarise, from the GrIP analysis, the geographical distribution of each of these segments. The strength of the approach outlined here is that it is framed around global reference points and around developed countries as much as developing countries, so it is global in its description. The weaknesses, of course, are that the cut-offs, even though they are based on reasoned justification, as set out above, are nevertheless somewhat subjective and therefore any estimates that are derived from them can be sensitive to where the cut-offs are located. For this reason, we present density curves and growth incidence curves for the entire global population, so that in addition to focusing on the different segments, readers can reflect on the implications of the global consumption distribution as a whole.

Using these groups or segments, we can ask who benefited and by how much from consumption growth since 1990. Figures 4.2, 4.3, 4.4 (and see also Table 5.1) show who benefited from growth in terms of the global growth incidence curve (with and without top income

Table 4.2 Where does each group live and how much do they consume? Data without top income adjustment

	Population (millions)					Consumption ($bn)					
	Destitute Less than $2	Poor Less than $4	Precariat $4–$10	Securiat $10–$30	Prosperiat $30+		Destitute Less than $2	Poor Less than $4	Precariat $4–$10	Securiat $10–$30	Prosperiat $30+
Total	956	2664	2030	1544	669		500	2331	4740	9622	14,757
China	84	360	579	372	39		50	359	1388	2099	654
India	292	907	291	35	4		170	815	596	188	60
East Asia and Pacific	134	577	832	571	152		81	571	1977	3390	2991
Europe and Central Asia	11	44	168	446	237		6	43	446	2990	4666
Latin America and Caribbean	59	165	212	177	43		30	145	514	1061	1070
Middle East and North Africa	3	52	177	138	28		2	59	440	812	513
North America	–	4	32	116	196		–	6	84	843	5249
South Asia Region	359	1148	439	57	5		208	1040	912	300	81
Sub-Saharan Africa	390	673	170	41	8		174	467	367	227	186

(continued)

Table 4.2 (continued)

	Population (millions)					Consumption ($bn)				
	Destitute Less than $2	Poor Less than $4	Precariat $4–$10	Securiat $10–$30	Prosperiat $30+	Destitute Less than $2	Poor Less than $4	Precariat $4–$10	Securiat $10–$30	Prosperiat $30+
E. Asia less China	49	218	252	199	113	30	213	589	1291	2337
S. Asia less India	67	242	148	21	1	38	225	316	111	21
High—OECD	1	13	104	451	483	0	15	279	3250	11,069
High—non-OECD	0	2	41	126	55	0	2	114	847	1112
LIC and MIC	955	2650	1886	967	131	500	2314	4346	5525	2576
UMIC	146	565	959	742	113	83	549	2330	4302	2267
LMIC	459	1469	816	209	17	257	1333	1788	1142	291
UMIC (excl. China)	62	205	379	370	74	32	190	943	2203	1613
LMIC (excl. India)	167	563	525	174	14	87	518	1191	953	231
LIC	350	616	110	15	1	160	432	229	81	18
LDCs	361	652	133	19	1	166	464	276	100	20
Fragile states (WB list)	146	247	80	33	3	60	166	178	185	45

Source GrIP v2.0

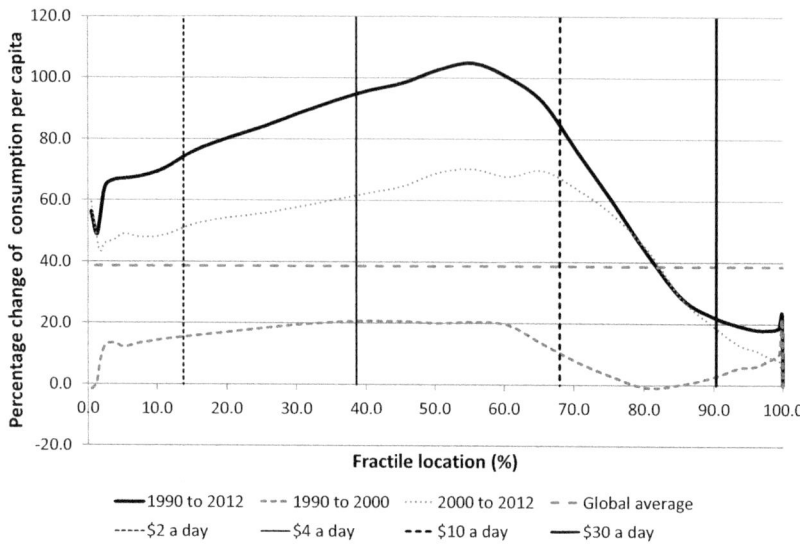

Fig. 4.2 Global growth incidence curve, 1990–2012, 1990–2000 and 2000–2012 *without* top income adjustment (*Source* GrIP v2.0)

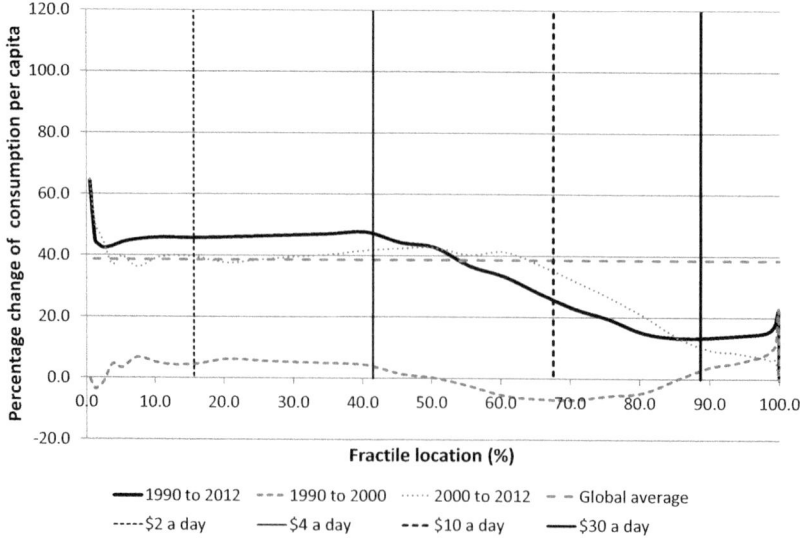

Fig. 4.3 Global growth incidence curve, excluding China, 1990–2012, 1990–2000 and 2000–2012, *without* top income adjustment (*Source* GrIP v2.0)

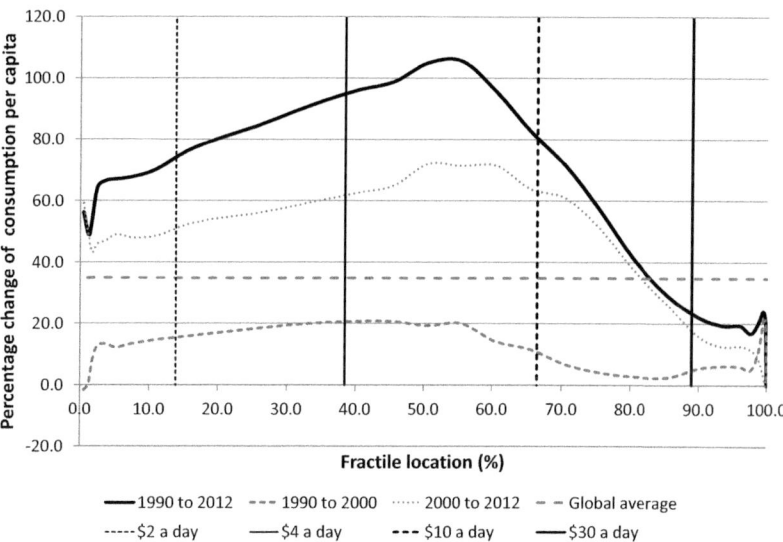

Fig. 4.4 Global growth incidence curve, 1990–2012, 1990–2000 and 2000–2012 *with* top income adjustment (*Source* GrIP v2.0)

adjustment). Data in the text are based on the estimates without top income adjustment. We find that those under $2 per day in 2012 had captured 1.9% of global consumption growth, 1990–2012. Those under $4 captured 9.4%. The precariat ($4–10) captured 20.3% while the securiat ($10–30) captured 31.1% and the prosperiat ($30+) captured 39.1% of global consumption growth.

These growth incidence curves provide further insight into the relative winners from global growth since 1990. Figures 4.2, 4.3, 4.4 show how people across the global consumption spectrum (from the poorest to the richest fractiles) have benefited in relative terms (i.e. percentage change in consumption from 1990 levels). People living in 2012 on between $2 and $10 a day had typically seen their per capita consumption levels rise, in percentage terms, by twice the global average or more. However, those on the higher consumption levels have seen their relative consumption rise more slowly than the global average so that *in relative terms* it is those with consumption levels at or above the top half of the securiat who have seen their consumption rise more slowly than global averages.

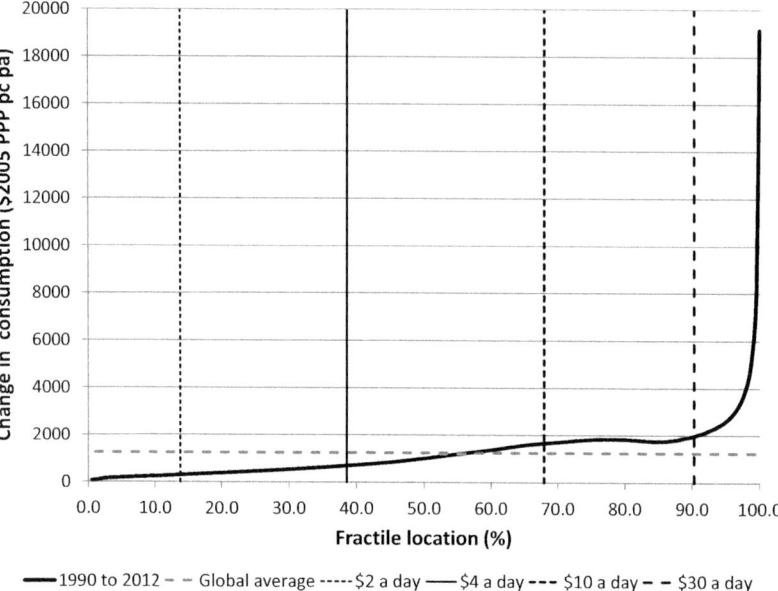

Fig. 4.5 Absolute change in consumption 1990–2012, *without* top income adjustment (*Source* GrIP v2.0)

However, the dominance of China underlying this picture can be starkly revealed. Once China is removed, the picture becomes very different with those living on less than $4 a day seeing their relative consumption rise much less, albeit nevertheless broadly in line with the global average (in percentage terms). At higher consumption levels, we find that the benefits of growth have not penetrated so far into the precariat and securiat. When China is excluded, we find that all those at or above the top half of the precariat have seen their relative consumption rise more slowly than the global average.

In this (relative) sense, the distribution of global growth since 1990 could be seen as having been generally pro-poor, even when China is excluded. However, it must be remembered that these relative consumption rises represent percentage changes on already very low consumption levels. When absolute consumption levels are considered the picture is, of course, very different (Figs. 4.5 and 4.6). Here it is the richest 40% who have seen their per capita consumption rise, in $-value, by more

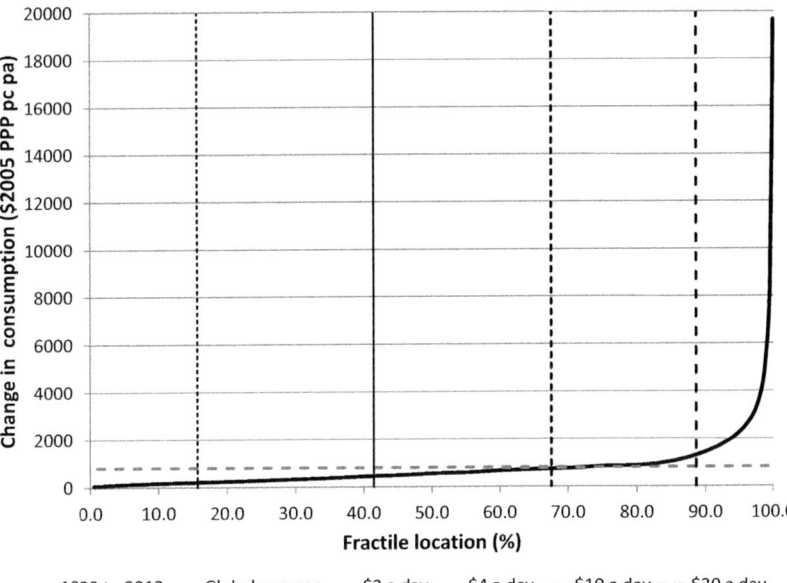

Fig. 4.6 Absolute change in consumption, excluding China, 1990–2012, *without* top income adjustment (*Source* GrIP v2.0)

than the global average, and with most of that benefit concentrated among those above $30 a day, the prosperiat. And if China is removed, then it is almost exclusively the prosperiat who have benefited by more than the global average.

Overall then, analysis of the distribution of the absolute benefits of global growth hardly seems to point to the emergence, within developing economies, of a burgeoning new secure 'middle'. There has though been a significant growth (1.1bn) in the number of people living secure from sliding back into poverty. There are now 2.2bn people in this 'global securiat' living above the $10 a day level. The 400mn of them who live in China have benefited enormously, as have the 700mn who constitute the world's richest decile. But the remaining 1.1bn of them have seen their consumption grow in absolute terms by less than the global average, and in relative terms by much less than (around 50% of) the global average since 1990.

In sum, far from witnessing a simplistic end to poverty in sight and the rise of a global 'middle class', we may well be witnessing something much more complex. A key dynamic is, unsurprisingly, the rapid transition of China on a trajectory towards becoming a more developed economy. This 'success story', however, can mask the fact that since 1990 the largest change in headcounts has been in the number of people globally living either in poverty, albeit not extreme poverty, or at risk of sliding back into poverty. Almost 80% of people in this group live outside China but the precarious nature of their existence is worth noting. And at higher consumption levels, among those secure from poverty, there is evidence that, other than for the world's top decile and for the 400mn people in China who are newly above the $10-a-day consumption level, the distribution of global growth since 1990 has seen them benefit by less than global averages in both absolute and relative terms.

As has been noted by many others, once the 'China effect' is disaggregated from the analysis, the much-heralded falls in extreme poverty may overstate the world's success in addressing global poverty, broadly defined, and be hypersensitive to where the line is drawn. This risks obscuring the very significant increase in the number of people in the world who, while above the extreme poverty line, are either still poor or at risk of sliding back into poverty. At higher consumption levels, among those living more securely (the global 'securiat' and 'prosperiat' above $10 a day), around half of them, those in the global top decile and those now living in China on more than $10 a day, have seen their consumption rise, in absolute terms, well above global averages. But for the rest of them, on average, they have seen their share of global consumption eroded, both in absolute and relative terms. The dominant narrative therefore risks obscuring a far less promising picture, of a burgeoning global middle who are insecure.

Global poverty levels at each of the three poverty lines we consider here ($2, $4 and $10) are presented as percentages of global population in Figs. 4.7 and 4.8 (with and without China respectively) and as absolute numbers (millions) in Figs. 4.9 and 4.10.

How robust and significant one considers the fall in global poverty to be depends on what line one uses, whether it includes China or not, and whether one considers proportion of population or total number of poor people. Figures 4.7 and 4.8 show that the falls in poverty tend to be more substantial as the poverty line falls. For example, at $10 per day, the fall in global poverty is just 10% over the period, falling from about 80% of the world's population to about 70%. If one excludes China, $10 poverty is about the same proportion of population in 2012 as it was in

4 GLOBAL POVERTY BY DIFFERENT POVERTY LINES SINCE THE COLD WAR   37

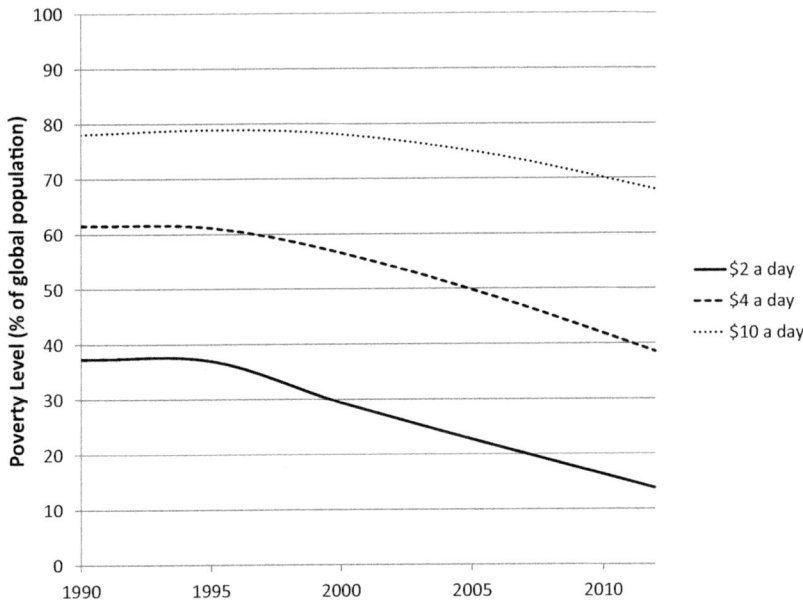

Fig. 4.7 Global poverty headcount (% of global population), 1990–2012 (*Source* GrIP v2.0)

1990. However, at $2 or $4 the fall is more substantial, respectively from 37 and 62% of world population in 1990 to 14 and 39% in 2012. Again, without China, the falls are much less impressive.

When one considers actual absolute numbers of people by each line, the record on poverty reduction further weakens drastically. Figures 4.9 and 4.10 show that even including China, $10 poverty has risen from 4 billion people to closer to 5 billion people, while $4 poverty is only slightly lower than it was in 1990 (3.1bn in 1990, 2.7bn in 2012). Poverty at the $2 line has fallen more convincingly if one includes China, effectively halving since 1990. However, with China excluded, at the $2 line, poverty has fallen much less impressively (from 1.2 billion people to just under 900 million) while at the $4 line, poverty headcounts in 2012 are still higher than 1990 (2.1 billion in 1990, 2.3 billion in 2012).

If one were to consider that the definition of being 'middle class' is to be sufficiently well off that you are secure from the risk of sliding into poverty

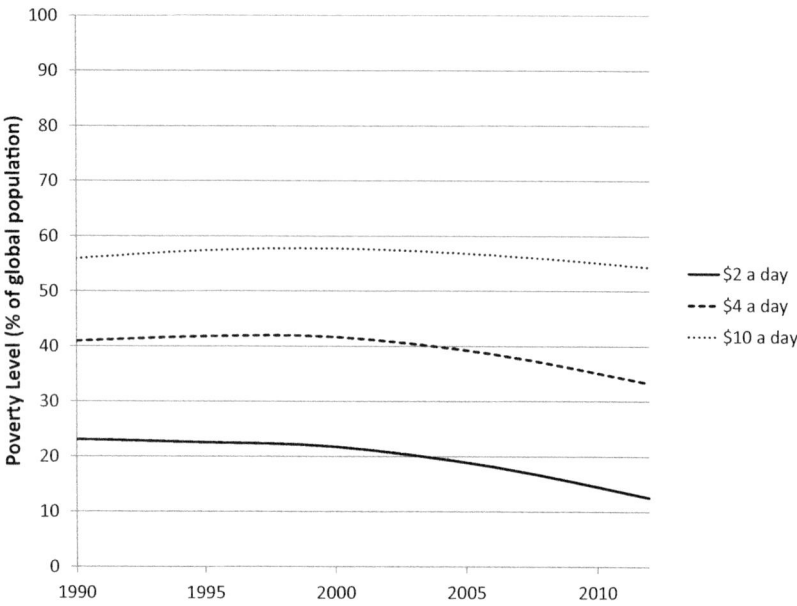

Fig. 4.8 Global poverty headcount (% of global population), excluding China, 1990–2012 (*Source* GrIP v2.0)

(and assume that that is achieved at consumption levels above $10 a day) then since 1990, an additional 1.1bn people have been added to this group, so there certainly has been a significant increase in the size of the global 'middle class'. However, at the same time, the number living above the destitution $2 poverty line but below the ($10) secure-from-poverty line has increased by 1.7bn. This group would include many people one might consider to still be very poor (living only a little above the extreme poverty line), plus those living precariously at risk of sliding back into poverty.

The total poverty gap gives a consistent picture to the above discussion (see Figs. 4.11 and 4.12). The global poverty gap at $10 rose over the last two decades but is now back to the point it was in 1990. At $4 per day the total poverty gap fell by approximately a third in value. The fall in the value of the total poverty gap at the lower lines is more substantial: at $2 and $4 per day, the total poverty gap fell in 2012 respectively to 40 and 64% of its value in 1990 ($493bn–$197bn at $2 and $2437bn to $1559bn at $4). However, when China is excluded, the $10 poverty

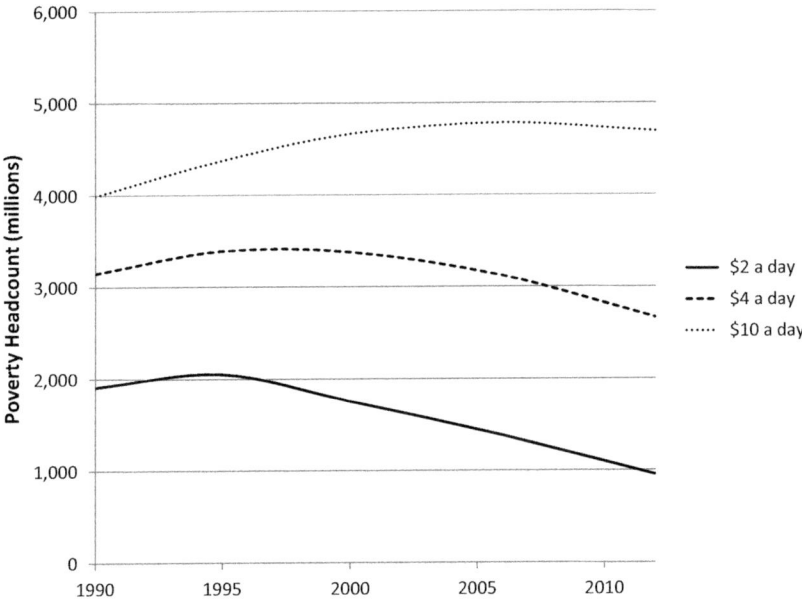

Fig. 4.9 Global poverty headcount (millions), 1990–2012 (*Source* GrIP v2.0)

gap has risen from $7150bn in 1990 to $8383bn in 2012. And the total poverty gap excluding China at the $4 poverty line is only slightly lower than in 1990 ($1561bn down to $1392bn) although the total poverty gap excluding China at $2 has fallen from $301bn to $186bn.

By focusing rather narrowly on the global success at reducing poverty against the very low extreme poverty line rather than lifting many people into a condition where they are newly secure from poverty, the dominant narrative rather obscures that in terms of absolute numbers the biggest change globally has been the increase in the size of the global poor and 'precariat' living on between $2 and $10 a day.

We should make clear that we are not dismissive of the progress that evidently has been made in terms of lowering poverty at very low poverty lines (such as $2 or the World Bank $1.90 extreme poverty line, and even when excluding China). Rather, we are noting that that decline is, of course, welcome, but that overall progress in poverty eradication is really rather more modest when one takes into account what has been happening at just slightly higher poverty lines. The real contention here

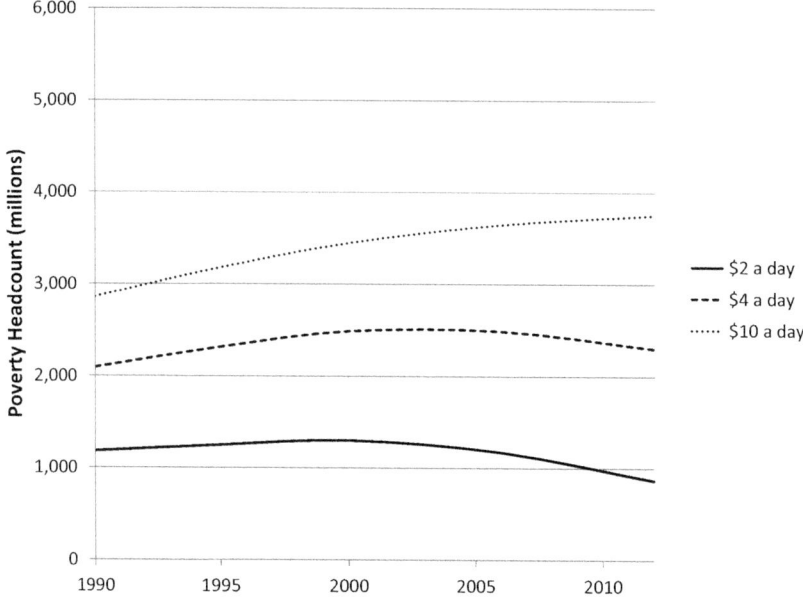

Fig. 4.10 Global poverty headcount (millions), excluding China, 1990–2012 (*Source* GrIP v2.0)

is, of course, whether anyone can live on consumption levels as low as $1.90 or $2, levels that Allen (2017) suggests are insufficient to meet basic needs in many developing countries.

To be clear, we are not saying that the world should not care about the poorest. What we are saying is that the world is not even counting some of the poorest. And we have argued thus far that very low poverty lines (such as $1.90 a day) generate poverty headcounts which are so hypersensitive that they create the impression that progress in the global battle against poverty has been more significant than it appears, when poverty lines that are both more globally representative and less sensitive (such as $4 a day) are applied. We suggest therefore that, far from witnessing a rapid reduction in global poverty and the emergence of a new 'middle class', most of the world's burgeoning middle is still very poor and highly precarious, in the sense that they live a considerable distance away from the consumption levels (e.g. $10 a day) associated with permanent escape from poverty in longitudinal surveys in developing countries.

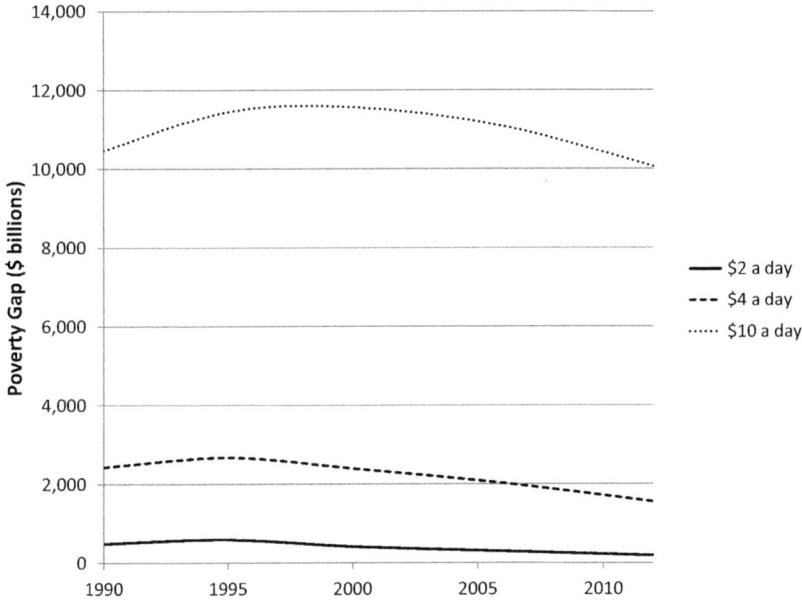

Fig. 4.11 Global poverty gap, 1990–2012 (US$bn, 2011 PPP) (*Source* GrIP v2.0)

This implies that, rather than focusing so much on the relationship between overall economic growth and extreme poverty headcounts, closer attention needs to be paid to the distribution of the benefits of growth. In Chapter 5, we therefore go on to consider how the increment in global growth from 1990 to 2012 was distributed, and how different the distribution of that increment would have needed to have been in order to have removed poverty already at the various different poverty lines. Our purpose here is not to suggest that such alternative distribution would have been easy to achieve. Instead, we want to discuss the fact that global consumption doubled in that period and yet despite this, global poverty persists on a large scale, and especially among those living slightly above extreme poverty levels. By considering what alternative distribution of the growth increment might have been required, our aim, therefore, is to present some context on just how challenging it might have been to eradicate poverty during the last two decades or so of tremendously increasing global prosperity. In doing so, we aim

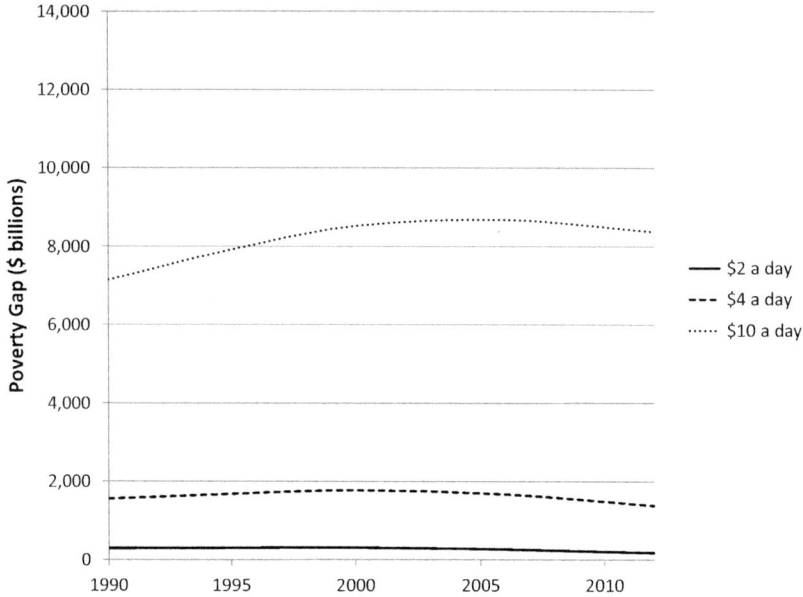

Fig. 4.12 Global poverty gap, excluding China, 1990–2012 (US$bn, 2011 PPP) (*Source* GrIP v2.0)

to bring into focus whether and to what degree different poverty lines imply different challenges to the forms of capitalism that have underpinned that growth. Or, in other words, is it sufficient to assume that the rising tide of economic growth can and will lift the poorest boats far enough to really eradicate poverty, or does poverty eradication necessitate a more radical approach to managing the distribution of the benefits of global growth?

REFERENCES

Allen, R. (2017). Absolute poverty: When necessity displaces desire. *American Economic Review, 107*(12), 3690–3721.

Banerjee, A., & Duflo, E. (2008). What is middle class about the middle classes around the world? *Journal of Economic Perspectives, 22*(2), 3–28.

Birdsall, N., Lustig, N., & Meyer, C. (2014). The strugglers: The new poor in Latin America. *World Development, 60*, 132–146.

Deaton, A. (2010). Price indexes, inequality, and the measurement of world poverty. *American Economic Review, 100*(1), 5–34.

Easterly, W. (2001). The middle class consensus and economic development. *Journal of Economic Growth, 6*(4), 317–355.

Edward, P., & Sumner, A. (2015). *New estimates of global poverty and inequality: How much difference do price data really make?* (Center for Global Development Working Paper 403). Washington, DC: CGD.

Edward, P., & Sumner, A. (2016). *Global inequality and global poverty since the cold war: How robust is the optimistic narrative?* (CROP Working Paper). Bergen: CROP/UiB.

Ferreira, F., Chen, S., & Dabalen, A. L., et al. (2015). *A global count of the extreme poor in 2012: Data issues, methodology, and initial results* (World Bank Working Paper). Washington DC: World Bank.

Ferreira, F., & Sanchez, C. (2017). *A richer array of international poverty lines*. Available at: http://blogs.worldbank.org/developmenttalk/richer-array-international-poverty-lines.

Jolliffe, D., & Prydz, E. (2015). *Global poverty goals and prices: How purchasing power parity matters* (World Bank Policy Research Working Paper 7256). Washington, DC: World Bank.

Kharas, H. (2010). *The emerging middle class in developing countries*. Paris: OECD Development Centre.

Lahoti, R., Jayadev, A., & Reddy, S. (2014). *The global consumption and income project (GCIP): An introduction and preliminary findings*. www.globalconsumptionandincomeproject.org. Accessed 4 June 2018.

Linder, S. B. (1961). *An essay on trade and transformation*. New York, NY: Wiley.

López-Calva, Luis F., & Ortiz-Juarez, E. (2014). A vulnerability approach to the definition of the middle class. *The Journal of Economic Inequality, 12*(1), 23–47.

Ravallion, M. (2002). *How not to count the poor? A reply to Reddy and Pogge*. Mimeo. Washington, DC: World Bank.

Ravallion, M. (2008). How not to count the poor? A reply to Reddy and Pogge. In S. Anand, P. Segal, & J. Stiglitz (Eds.), *Debates on the measurement of poverty*. Oxford: Oxford University Press.

Ravallion, M. (2010). The developing world's bulging (but vulnerable) middle class. *World Development, 38*(4), 445–454.

Reddy, S., & Pogge, T. (2002). *How not to count the poor* (version 3.0). Mimeo. New York: Barnard College.

Reddy, S., & Pogge, T. (2005). *How not to count the poor* (version 6.2). Mimeo. New York: Barnard College.

Standing, G. (2011). *The Precariat: The new dangerous class*. London: Bloomsbury Academic.

Sumner, A. (2016). *Global poverty*. Oxford: Oxford University Press.
Sumner, A., Yusuf, A., & Suara, Y. (2014). The prospects of the poor: A set of poverty measures based on the probability of remaining poor (or not) in Indonesia. *Working Papers in Economics and Development Studies (WoPEDS) from Department of Economics*, Padjadjaran University.

CHAPTER 5

The End of Global Poverty

Abstract In this chapter, we discuss the following question: What amount of redistribution of the growth increment would have been necessary to have ended poverty at various poverty lines? We find that the data point to significant implications on the role of global economic growth in the eradication of poverty.

Keywords Poverty · Inequality · Growth

Next we discuss the following question: what amount of redistribution of the growth increment would have been necessary to have ended poverty at various poverty lines? The data point to significant implications on the role of global economic growth in the eradication of poverty. Our findings show that quite different forms of capitalism are required to end poverty at the different poverty lines. Each of the three different poverty lines ($2, $4 and $10 a day, see Table 5.1) implies a very different degrees of challenge to the way the global economy works and how the benefits of economic growth are distributed.

If we first consider the lowest poverty line, we find that those under $2 poverty benefited from just 1.9% of the global consumption increment (from 1990 to 2012). If instead they had captured 3.3% of that global increment, the world would have eliminated poverty at this poverty line. If the global aspiration had been to remove the poverty of the destitute (those living on less than $2), then it would have required only

© The Author(s) 2019
P. Edward and A. Sumner, *The End of Poverty*,
https://doi.org/10.1007/978-3-030-14764-8_5

Table 5.1 Estimates of scale of redistribution of the growth increment, 1990–2012 to eradicate poverty: Data with and without top income adjustment

	Poor		Poor+Precariat	Precariat	Securiat	Prosperiat	Total
	Destitute: less than $2	Absolute: less than $4	Less than $10	$4–$10	$10–$30	$30+	
Without top income adjustment							
Population in fractile in 2012 (millions)	956	2664	4695	2030	1544	669	6908
Fractile percentage in 2012	13.8	38.6	68.0	29.4	22.4	9.7	100.0
2012 consumption of segment ($bn)	500	2331	7071	4740	9622	14,757	31,450
1990 population (million) for same share of population as in 2012	707	1971	3473	1502	1143	495	5111
1990 consumption upper cut-off level ($/year) for same population share as in 2012	417	750	1970		9020		
Consumption of global segment in 1990 ($bn)	220	948	2709	1761	5056	9021	16,785
Consumption growth of segment 1990–2012 ($bn)	280	1383	4362	2979	4566	5736	14,664
Segment's share of global consumption growth 1990–2012 (%)	1.9	9.4	29.7	20.3	31.1	39.1	100.0
Poverty gap in 2012 ($bn)	197	1559	10,065				
Share of global consumption growth 1990–2012 that would have 'ended poverty' to top of the segment (%)	3.3	20.1	98.4				
With top income adjustment							
Population in fractile in 2012 (millions)	956	2658	4596	1938	1550	763	6908
Fractile percentage in 2012	13.8	38.5	66.5	28.0	22.4	11.0	100.0
2012 consumption of segment ($bn)	500	2324	6840	4516	9639	23,518	39,997

(continued)

Table 5.1 (continued)

	Poor		Poor+Precariat	Precariat	Securiat	Prosperiat	Total
	Destitute: less than $2	Absolute: less than $4	Less than $10	$4–$10	$10–$30	$30+	
1990 population (million) for same share of population as in 2012	707	1967	3400	1434	1147	564	5111
1990 consumption upper cut-off level ($/year) for same population share as in 2012	417	749	2028		8813		
Consumption of global segment in 1990 ($bn)	220	945	2637	1692	4972	14,332	21,941
Consumption growth of segment 1990–2012 ($bn)	280	1379	4202	2824	4667	9186	18,056
Segment's share of global consumption growth 1990–2012 (%)	1.6	7.6	23.3	15.6	25.8	50.9	100.0
Poverty gap in 2012 ($bn)	197	1557	9935				
Share of global consumption growth 1990–2012 that would have 'ended poverty' to top of the segment (%)	2.6	16.3	78.3				

Source GrIP v2.0

an extra 1.4% of the 1990–2012 global growth to have been redistributed to the poor.

Had this money been redirected away from the prosperiat, then they would have seen *their share of the global consumption growth* in that period fall just very slightly from 39.1 to 37.7%. One might therefore refer to this scenario as something akin to *global philanthropy*, although while the additional reallocation of growth required might seem rather modest, it is worth noting that it still represents a 75% increase in the share of consumption accruing to the destitute, which potentially implies that existing mechanisms for ensuring the poor benefit from growth may not be adequate to achieve even this modest amount of redistribution.

Eradicating poverty by 2012 at the $4 poverty line would have been considerably more challenging, requiring much more substantial reallocation of growth benefits towards the poorest. Those under $4 captured 9.4% of global consumption growth since 1990, but to have eradicated poverty at this level, they would have needed to capture 20.1% of that growth increment. This is evidently a much more challenging reallocation as, if it was all reallocated from the prosperiat, then that would lead to a sizeable reduction in their share of global growth.

Rather than the modest reallocation of the global philanthropy scenario that could have removed destitution poverty by clawing back the share of the growth accruing to the prosperiat from 39% to just under 38%, eradicating absolute $4 poverty would have required their share to fall to 28%. Such a reduction would probably still support the logic—the motivating force of individual interest and reward—that underpins capitalism. But it implies a sufficiently different and interventionist mode of distribution of the benefits of growth which merits some consideration of how much redistribution of the growth increment—from whom and to whom—would have been needed, and what this might imply for understanding how that reallocation might impact the modality of capitalism pursued.

To investigate this, we develop here a model of redistribution as an analytical device that helps to illustrate these issues. This requires us to make a number of assumptions. First, we consider that since consumption growth was around ten times the $4 poverty gap, there should be no need for anyone to be poorer in 2012 than in 1990. In fact, we assume that everyone—from richest to poorest—should be able to benefit from that growth. So, we only consider redistribution of the shares of the consumption growth increment. Second, we consider, for now, only the analysis without the top income adjustment, on the basis that this is the more challenging scenario, since there is less growth to redistribute globally and so the shares of growth to be foregone are larger (we return later to consideration of the significance of the top income adjustment).

Third, we assume that it is only those in the global prosperiat who will contribute to the redistribution, and we cap the maximum redistribution that anyone might be expected to contribute to 50% of their growth in average per capita consumption. In this way, we aim to explore whether it would have been possible to eradicate poverty at different poverty lines over the 1990–2012 period, while still retaining substantial returns to the prosperiat in order to maintain to a reasonable degree the incentives of individual gain that capitalism relies on for its motivating drive.

The preceding calculation is made separately for each country to ensure that having allowed for differences in consumption and population growth rates, no-one in the prosperiat in any country is expected to contribute more than 50% of their consumption per capita growth. This country-by-country approach is an important methodological clarification designed to ensure that the analysis takes account of differences in national consumption and population growth rates and initial consumption per capita levels. Overall, at the global level, this country-by-country approach and the 50% cap on the contribution of the prosperiat ensures that even after redistribution, the global prosperiat would still see their consumption levels rise by more per capita in absolute terms than would the securiat. In other words, we consider a level of redistribution that would merely dilute rather than invert the differential incentives, whereby the greatest absolute rewards accrue to the richest (we are not arguing that this is how the global economic system must or should work, but merely observing that this is how it does work currently, and our aim here is to develop a scenario that does not require an inversion of that logic while still accounting for the necessary scale of reallocation of the benefits of growth if poverty is to be eradicated at different poverty lines).

Finally, we assume that the issue of redistribution is first and foremost a national one. So, we assume that wherever possible, money available for redistribution (on the basis of the preceding assumptions) is reallocated first to remove in-country poverty, with any balance then remaining being available to contribute to global (international) redistribution. This means that in a middle-income country (MIC) such as China, those in the prosperiat would contribute first to removing poverty in China at the rate of 50% of their share of global growth. Any balance remaining after that within-country redistribution would then contribute to a global 'pot', but since that would not (at the $2 and $4 poverty lines we are considering here) be called on in full, the effective call on that money would be less than the 50% rate. What this means is that in our analysis the burden of eradicating poverty in a given country falls more heavily on members of the prosperiat living in that country than it does on the global community, something that we find not unreasonable, and consistent with the notion that one of the purposes of national economic growth is to remove national poverty.

We propose this model of redistribution as an analytical device based on reasonable assumptions that can help to expose where and by how much the burden of successfully eradicating poverty by 2012 might have fallen. Results for our analysis are provided in Table 5.2 for $2 poverty and Table 5.3 for $4 poverty. We discuss $4 first and then $2 poverty because, as noted earlier, the latter is far less challenging. We find that, out of 171 countries for which adequate data exist (in both 1990 and 2012) to make the calculations, in 138 countries there is some $4 poverty. Fifty of these countries could have ended that poverty via within-country redistribution of the growth increment without needing any transnational transfers (see Table 5.3). This would have reduced global $4 poverty by 532m people.

The remaining 88 countries would have needed some transnational transfer. Within-country redistribution (both in the 50 countries that could remove poverty without transnational assistance and in those that need such assistance, on the basis that they transfer first as much as they can internally and then the international community makes up the rest) would redistribute $307bn from the richest segment (the prosperiat, above $30 in 2012) to the poorest. After this redistribution, there would still be a remaining global shortfall of $1220bn needing to be covered by transnational redistribution, and there would be $1581bn available for such transnational transfers. So, in effect, the world could (just, the cover ratio for global transfers is 77.2%=1220/1581) have 'afforded' to remove $4 poverty by 2012 (on the basis of all the assumptions outlined above).

Which countries are we talking about? Eleven OECD HIC countries have $4 poverty, but they can all afford to remove this themselves. Twenty-seven LICs have $4 poverty but none could afford to remove it all themselves. About half of the MICs could have ended $4 poverty

Table 5.2 Estimates of scale of redistribution of the growth increment, 1990–2012 to eradicate $2 poverty, *without* top income adjustment

	Amount available for within-country global transfers ($bn)	No. of countries that can afford to remove poverty without global transfers	No. of countries that require global transfers	Total poverty headcount (millions)	Poverty headcount in countries that can afford to remove poverty without global transfers (mills)	Amount transferred within-country ($bn)	Poverty gap remaining after within-country transfers ($bn)	Total available for global transfers ($bn)	Amount received in global transfer ($bn)	Amount provided to global transfer ($bn)	Total amount transferred (within-country and global) ($bn)	Cover ratio (% all transfers)
Total	1888.1	43	62	935	172	50.8	142.2	1837.3	142.2	142.2	193.1	10.2
China	271.5	1	0	84	84	11.3	0.0	260.2	0.0	20.1	31.4	11.6
India	18.3	0	1	292	0	18.3	24.4	0.0	24.4	0.0	18.3	100.0
East Asia and Pacific	629.5	9	9	131	110	14.9	1.9	614.6	1.9	47.6	62.5	9.9
Europe and Central Asia	522.8	3	8	11	1	0.1	2.4	522.7	2.4	40.5	40.6	7.8
Latin America and Caribbean	175.0	24	4	54	49	10.9	1.0	164.1	1.0	12.7	23.7	13.5
Middle East and North Africa	25.7	2	1	3	3	0.3	0.0	25.4	0.0	2.0	2.2	8.7
North America	466.7	0	0	0	0	0.0	0.0	466.7	0.0	36.1	36.1	7.7
South Asia Region	24.0	0	3	351	0	18.4	34.2	5.5	34.2	0.4	18.9	78.8
Sub-Saharan Africa	44.4	5	37	385	9	6.2	102.8	38.2	102.8	3.0	9.1	20.6

(continued)

Table 5.2 (continued)

	Amount available for within-country global transfers ($bn)	No. of countries that can afford to remove poverty without global transfers	No. of countries that require global transfers	Total poverty headcount (millions)	Poverty headcount in countries that can afford to remove poverty without global transfers (mills)	Amount transferred within-country ($bn)	Poverty gap remaining after within-country transfers ($bn)	Total available for global transfers ($bn)	Amount received in global transfer ($bn)	Amount provided to global transfer ($bn)	Total amount transferred (within-country and global) ($bn)	Cover ratio (% all transfers)
E. Asia less China	358.0	8	9	47	25	3.6	1.9	354.4	1.9	27.4	31.0	8.7
S. Asia less India	5.6	0	2	59	0	0.1	9.8	5.5	9.8	0.4	0.6	9.8
High–OECD	1100.6	2	0	1	1	0.1	0.0	1100.5	0.0	85.2	85.3	7.8
High–non-OECD	169.8	8	0	0	0	0.0	0.0	169.8	0.0	13.1	13.2	7.8
LIC and MIC	617.6	33	62	934	171	50.7	142.2	566.9	142.2	43.9	94.6	15.3
UMIC	541.5	20	10	146	136	21.6	2.7	519.9	2.7	40.3	61.8	11.4
LMIC	74.7	13	25	457	35	27.7	49.9	47.0	49.9	3.6	31.3	42.0
UMIC (excl. China)	270.0	19	10	62	52	10.3	2.7	259.7	2.7	20.1	30.4	11.3
LMIC (excl. India)	56.4	13	24	166	35	9.4	25.5	47.0	25.5	3.6	13.0	23.1
LIC	1.4	0	27	331	0	1.4	89.7	0.0	89.7	0.0	1.4	100.0
LDCs	2.9	3	35	342	3	2.6	91.2	0.3	91.2	0.0	2.6	90.3
Fragile states	0.4	2	19	128	3	0.3	42.0	0.1	42.0	0.0	0.4	85.8

Source GrIP v2.0

Table 5.3 Estimates of scale of redistribution of the growth increment, 1990–2012 to eradicate $4 poverty, *without* top income adjustment

	Amount available for within-country global transfers ($bn)	No. of countries that can afford to remove poverty without global transfers	No. of countries that require global transfers	Total poverty headcount (millions)	Poverty headcount in countries that can afford to remove poverty without global transfers (mills)	Amount transferred within-country ($bn)	Poverty gap remaining after within-country transfers ($bn)	Total available for global transfers ($bn)	Amount received in global transfer ($bn)	Amount provided to global transfer ($bn)	Total amount transferred (within-country and global) ($bm)	Cover ratio (%, all transfers)
Total	1888.1	50	88	2612	532	306.8	1220.2	1581.3	1220.2	1220.2	1527.0	80.9
China	271.5	1	0	360	360	166.9	0.0	104.6	0.0	80.7	247.6	91.2
India	18.3	0	1	907	0	18.3	490.0	0.0	490.0	0.0	18.3	100.0
East Asia and Pacific	629.5	9	14	567	386	186.9	79.4	442.6	79.4	341.5	528.4	83.9
Europe and Central Asia	522.8	12	11	44	11	3.8	17.8	519.0	17.8	400.5	404.3	77.3
Latin America and Caribbean	175.0	19	13	157	91	69.9	19.3	105.1	19.3	81.1	151.0	86.3
Middle East and North Africa	25.7	4	5	50	14	4.8	12.2	20.9	12.2	16.1	20.9	81.4
North America	466.7	1	0	4	4	0.7	0.0	466.0	0.0	359.5	360.3	77.2

(continued)

Table 5.3 (continued)

	Amount available for without-in-country and global transfers ($bn)	No. of countries that can afford to remove poverty without global transfers	No. of countries that require global transfers	Total poverty headcount (millions)	Poverty headcount in countries that can afford to remove poverty without global transfers (mills)	Amount transferred with-in-country ($bn)	Poverty gap remaining after with-in-country transfers ($bn)	Total available for global transfers ($bn)	Amount received in global transfer ($bn)	Amount provided to global transfer ($bn)	Total amount transferred (with-in-country and global) ($bn)	Cover ratio (%, all transfers)
South Asia Region	24.0	2	4	1124	4	22.6	599.9	1.4	599.9	1.1	23.6	98.7
Sub-Saharan Africa	44.4	3	41	667	21	18.0	491.6	26.4	491.6	20.3	38.4	86.4
E. Asia less China	358.0	8	14	207	26	20.0	79.4	338.0	79.4	260.8	280.8	78.4
S. Asia less India	5.6	2	3	217	4	4.2	109.9	1.4	109.9	1.1	5.3	94.3
High—OECD	1100.6	11	0	13	13	3.5	0.0	1097.1	0.0	846.5	850.1	77.2
High—non-OECD	169.8	12	2	2	2	0.8	0.1	169.1	0.1	130.5	131.2	77.3
LIC and MIC	617.6	27	86	2598	518	302.5	1220.1	315.1	1220.1	243.2	545.7	88.3
UMIC	541.5	19	23	563	482	247.6	27.8	294.0	27.8	226.8	474.4	87.6
LMIC	74.7	8	36	1467	36	53.5	757.1	21.2	757.1	16.3	69.8	93.5

(continued)

Table 5.3 (continued)

	Amount available for within-country and global transfers ($bn)	No. of countries that can afford to remove poverty without global transfers	No. of countries that require global transfers	Total poverty headcount (millions)	Poverty headcount in countries that can afford to remove poverty without global transfers (mills)	Amount transferred within-country ($bn)	Poverty gap remaining after within-country transfers ($bn)	Total available for global transfers ($bn)	Amount received in global transfer ($bn)	Amount provided to global transfer ($bn)	Total amount transferred (within-country and global) ($bn)	Cover ratio (%, all transfers)
UMIC (excl. China)	270.0	18	23	204	122	80.7	27.8	189.3	27.8	146.1	226.8	84.0
LMIC (excl. India)	56.4	8	35	560	36	35.2	267.1	21.2	267.1	16.3	51.5	91.4
LIC	1.4	0	27	567	0	1.4	435.2	0.0	435.2	0.0	1.4	100.0
LDCs	2.9	2	37	602	0	2.8	453.2	0.1	453.2	0.0	2.9	99.6
Fragile states	0.4	0	21	205	0	0.4	166.9	0.0	166.9	0.0	0.4	100.0

Source GrIP v2.0

Table 5.4 Estimates of scale of redistribution of the growth increment, 1990–2012 to eradicate $10 poverty, *without* top income adjustment

	Amount available for within-country and global transfers ($bn)	No. of countries that can afford to remove poverty without global transfers	No. of countries that require global transfers	Total poverty headcount (millions)	Poverty headcount in countries that can afford to remove poverty without global transfers (mills)	Amount transferred within-country ($bn)	Poverty gap remaining after within-country transfers ($bn)	Total available for global transfers ($bn)	Amount received in global transfer ($bn)	Amount provided to global transfer ($bn)	Total amount transferred (within-country and global) ($bn)	Cover ratio (%, all transfers)
Total	1888.1	39	130	4610	147	743.0	9135.6	1145.1	1145.1	1145.1	1888.1	100.0
China	271.5	0	1	939	0	271.5	1411.0	0.0	176.9	0.0	271.5	100.0
India	18.3	0	1	1198	0	18.3	2941.3	0.0	368.7	0.0	18.3	100.0
East Asia and Pacific	629.5	8	18	1394	33	347.4	2210.4	282.2	277.0	282.2	629.5	100.0
Europe and Central Asia	522.8	23	20	210	71	97.8	185.2	425.0	23.2	425.0	522.8	100.0
Latin America and Caribbean	175.0	2	30	367	3	171.9	516.0	3.2	64.7	3.2	175.0	100.0
Middle East and North Africa	25.7	3	12	209	3	13.5	301.9	12.2	37.8	12.2	25.7	100.0
North America	466.7	3	0	37	37	44.1	0.0	422.6	0.0	422.6	466.7	100.0
South Asia Region	24.0	0	6	1558	0	24.0	3742.6	0.0	469.1	0.0	24.0	100.0
Sub-Saharan Africa	44.4	0	44	837	0	44.4	2179.5	0.0	273.2	0.0	44.4	100.0
E. Asia less China	358.0	8	17	454	33	75.8	799.4	282.2	100.2	282.2	358.0	100.0

(continued)

Table 5.4 (continued)

	Amount available for within-country and global transfers ($bn)	No. of countries that can afford to remove poverty without global transfers	No. of countries that require global transfers	Total poverty headcount (millions)	Poverty headcount in countries that can afford to remove poverty without global transfers (mills)	Amount transferred within-country ($bn)	Poverty gap remaining after within-country transfers ($bn)	Total available for global transfers ($bn)	Amount received in global transfer ($bn)	Amount provided to global transfer ($bn)	Total amount transferred (within-country and global) ($bn)	Cover ratio (%, all transfers)
S. Asia less India	5.6	0	5	360	0	5.6	801.3	0.0	100.4	0.0	5.6	100.0
High—OECD	1100.6	25	4	116	85	119.6	10.2	981.0	1.3	981.0	1100.6	100.0
High—non-OECD	169.8	8	13	42	32	32.3	9.0	137.6	1.1	137.6	169.8	100.0
LIC and MIC	617.6	6	113	4452	29	591.2	9116.4	26.5	1142.7	26.5	617.6	100.0
UMIC	541.5	5	42	1506	19	520.2	2142.7	21.4	268.6	21.4	541.5	100.0
LMIC	74.7	1	44	2280	10	69.6	5140.9	5.1	644.4	5.1	74.7	100.0
UMIC (excl. China)	270.0	5	41	567	19	248.6	731.7	21.4	91.7	21.4	270.0	100.0
LMIC (excl. India)	56.4	1	43	1082	10	51.3	2199.6	5.1	275.7	5.1	56.4	100.0
LIC	1.4	0	27	666	0	1.4	1832.8	0.0	229.7	0.0	1.4	100.0
LDCs	2.9	0	39	723	0	2.9	1960.3	0.0	245.7	0.0	2.9	100.0
Fragile states	0.4	0	21	258	0	0.4	697.2	0.0	87.4	0.0	0.4	100.0

Source GrIP v2.0

without the help of transnational transfers. While the cover ratio for global transfers would be 77.2%, once all the within-country transfers are taken into account, the overall cover ratio (the percentage of total available funds redistributed both within-country and globally) would be 80.9%.

For China, for example, the effective cover ratio would be 91.2%, reflecting the assumption in the analysis that China would both fully fund redistribution internally, plus contribute to global transfers at 77.2% of any remaining balance of its transfer funds. Countries such as the LICs, that cannot afford to remove poverty alone, have a cover ratio of 100%, reflecting that in this analysis, it is assumed that all their estimated transfer funds are redistributed within-country, in addition to receiving global transfers.

These differences reflect the underlying assumption in our analysis that countries should do what they can to help themselves before having recourse to global transfers. We are *not* proposing this 'help yourself before the world helps you' approach as a policy recommendation. All we want to demonstrate is that the assumptions built into our analysis first place the burden of poverty alleviation on national populations, and only second on the international community. And yet, even with those assumptions, the analysis estimates that 80% (1220/1527) of the poverty eradication redistribution would need to be in the form of global transfers and about two-thirds of the total global redistribution (64.2% = [850 + 131]/1527) would need to come from HICs. Even after several decades of substantial global economic growth, in which some developing and emerging economies have enjoyed unprecedented growth rates and substantial poverty reduction, the challenge of global poverty still remains one to which the richer countries of the world would need to make a very strong commitment if the aspiration was to eradicate $4 poverty.

Results for $2 poverty are provided in Table 5.2. These confirm, as discussed earlier, that the challenge of eradicating poverty at this destitution level would be much lower than at $4. Although 105 countries have poverty at the $2 rate, using the assumptions in this analysis, 43 of those countries could eradicate that poverty through within-country transfers, and the overall cover ratio would be just 10.2%. The contribution of the HICs would fall to less than 10% of the funds assumed available from the prosperiat and would amount to just half of the total global redistribution burden.

In summary then, we might say that despite strong global economic growth in the period from 1990 to 2012, the pattern and distribution of that growth was nowhere near as 'poverty efficient' as it might have been. If, on average, the richest population decile (the prosperiat consuming $30 or more a day) had 'merely' foregone 5% of their increase in consumption over that period (10.2% of 50%—recall the assumption earlier that only 50% of the increase is potentially available for redistribution), we could today be living in a world free from $2 poverty. The $2 poverty line is, however, very low. Removing poverty at the more reasonable poverty line of $4 would have been rather more challenging as it would have entailed redistributing a much larger share of global growth to those living on under $4 a day. To achieve this, the prosperiat would have had to forego 40% of their increase in consumption (80.9% of 50%). This would doubtless have been very challenging, especially as it would have required substantial reallocation of the benefits of growth away from HICs, and towards LICs and MICs.

However, if there had been a system of global social welfare in place, it might still have been achievable. We term this *global social welfare* because although it entails large-scale redistributions from rich to poor, it would still have meant that on average, the prosperiat would have seen their average per capita consumption level grow in absolute terms by around twice that of the securiat. There is, therefore, reason to suppose that this level of redistribution might, in theory, be achieved by diluting rather than inverting the logic of differential incentives in liberal capitalism, whereby the greatest absolute rewards accrue to the richest.

However, it is likely that to expect the prosperiat to forego such a large share of the growth that they enjoyed in the 1990–2012 period would have required very considerable political contestation (particularly given that even the far more modest redistribution required to remove $2 poverty by 2012 does not seem to have been achievable). This *global social welfare* scenario might therefore be thought of as requiring substantial changes in the governance of growth and its distribution across consumption levels, so that removing absolute ($4) poverty might be regarded as needing a welfarist form of capitalism of a scale not yet visible in the world.

If the world had aspired in the period 1990–2012, to the challenge of creating a world in which no one had to live at risk of sliding back into poverty by removing poverty at $10 a day, then it would have been necessary to ensure that all of the economic growth that accrued not only to the prosperiat but also to the securiat was redistributed to the poor and the precariat. Results for the $10 poverty line (Table 5.4) reveal that to remove the precariat group's risk of sliding back into poverty would require a global transfer fund of almost $10 trillion, more than five times the maximum size that our analysis assumes is available from the prosperiat. This implies that removing poverty at the $10-a-day level would have required a pattern of global growth that yielded negligible growth in consumption among not only the prosperiat, but also the securiat in order to concentrate all the benefits of growth on the poor and the precariat.

In marked contrast to the global welfare challenge of $4 poverty, removing poverty at $10 would therefore necessitate an inversion of the dominant logic of capitalism; namely, that while most of the benefits of growth accrue to the non-poor, nevertheless, the trickledown of a smaller share of global growth to those on lower consumption levels can ultimately eradicate poverty. Indeed, this is such an inversion of that normal logic of capitalism that it is difficult to envisage how such a situation could be achieved without a radically different form of global economic organisation.

The discussion above indicates how focusing on poverty without considering the distributional dimensions can leave one blind to the political challenges to the existing global economic order implied by an aspiration to 'make poverty history'. In short, $2 poverty could have been eradicated by now through very modest (but not necessarily easily achieved) redistribution of global growth since 1990, in what might be labelled as a scenario of global philanthropy. In contrast, ending $4 poverty would have required a scenario that requires substantial intervention in terms of—presumably—global and national social welfare regimes to shift the benefits of growth both within and between countries. Ending $10 poverty would have required some sort of radically different global economic model.

What difference would it make if one uses data adjusted for top incomes? (see data in Tables 7.2, 7.3, and 7.4). The top income adjustment increases the amount of global consumption growth in the analysis from $14.7tn to $18.1tn, and the share of this growth that is captured by the prosperiat increases from 39.1 to 50.9%. Not surprisingly, the scenario of removing destitute ($2) poverty (Table 7.2) remains one of philanthropy as the global transfer cover ratio falls to 6.2% (from 10.2% without the top income adjustment). Eradicating absolute ($4) poverty also becomes easier with the cover ratio falling to 48.6% (from 80.9%)—a significant difference but hardly sufficient difference to reduce the problem of poverty eradication from one of global social welfare regimes to one of merely more philanthropy (see Table 7.3).

These results are not particularly surprising. What is perhaps more interesting is whether, once the top income adjustment is made, there is a possibility that the world could have removed the risk of sliding back into poverty ($10) through global social welfare (see Table 7.4). Here we find that it would still be necessary to redistribute more than three times the assumed global transfer fund available from the prosperiat. In other words, and bearing in mind that this fund is assumed to be 50% of the prosperiat group's consumption growth share, even after allowing for the top incomes adjustment, it would still be necessary for redistribution to extend deeply into the share of the securiat. This is consistent with the data in Table 5.1 that shows that 78.3% of global consumption growth would have needed to be redistributed to those on $10 or less, reducing the share captured by the securiat and prosperiat from 76.7% to just 21.7%.

In other words, even with adjustment for missing top incomes, we still find that in order to have removed poverty at the $10 level in the 1990–2012 period, 80% of the growth would have had to accrue to the poorest 70% of the global population, while just 20% accrued to the richest 30%. This remains the inversion of the dominant capitalist logic that we identified earlier, so even after making allowance for the possibility that top incomes are not adequately captured in the national household survey data, we still see the eradication of $10 poverty (and so by implication a move to a world where everyone is free from the risk of sliding back into poverty) as likely to require a radically different form of economic organisation (Tables 5.2, 5.3, and 5.4).

CHAPTER 6

Conclusion

Abstract In this chapter, we conclude that the causes of the persistence of global absolute poverty, certainly at $2 and $4 per day, and its eventual elimination are less due to insufficient consumption growth overall than to the pattern of growth or the distribution of the growth increment which has not been conducive to eliminating poverty at $2 or $4. Eradicating $2 poverty may require some enhanced tax and transfers, but eradicating $4 poverty would require a substantial shift towards stronger welfare regimes. This implies that a much greater focus in policy is needed on the governance of growth—managing the pattern of growth and who benefits—if $2 or $4 poverty are to be ended. And if $10 poverty were to be ended in coming decades, a radically new form of economic organisation is needed.

Keywords Poverty · Inequality · Growth

In this book, we have sought to develop a global perspective on the interaction of growth, poverty and inequality in order to bring greater clarity to the challenge of ending global poverty: a challenge that persists despite living in a world that is richer than ever before. Global output and consumption effectively doubled from 1990 to 2012 (when measured in PPP terms) and the number of people who lived below the lowest poverty lines certainly fell dramatically. Even so, one in seven people still live on less than $2 a day and one in three on less than $4 a day (in

2011 PPP). We argue that, given there was some $15 trillion of consumption growth in that period and that the remaining poverty gaps at $2 and $4 are respectively $200bn and $1.6tn, the persistence of global poverty (at least at the lower lines) cannot be fully explained by 'insufficient growth' in overall consumption. We argue instead that it is the *efficiency* by which that consumption growth has been translated into poverty reduction which is of significance. This finding is particularly relevant and challenging to the aspiration, central to the United Nations SDGs, to end global poverty 'in all its forms' by 2030.

This book has analysed the distribution of the consumption growth noted above and, from that, has discussed the scale of the challenge implied in ending global poverty at various poverty lines. The approach we took was to assess different ways that the growth since 1990 could have been distributed more efficiently, in terms of its poverty-reducing impact. This is, of course, hypothetical. We make no claims about political feasibility. However, we were careful to construct a model which redistributed the *growth increment* in a manner that would ensure that any redistribution assumed in the model would still maintain capitalism's logic—incentives for growth—across the entire global distribution. In other words, we have not assumed that the richer people of the world would suddenly relinquish, in favour of the poor, their claim to a large share of global growth. Instead, the model asks the questions, 'What if it had been possible to reallocate the distribution of the growth increment more efficiently as a route to poverty reduction?', and 'How much reallocation would have been needed to ensure there was plenty, or at least enough, growth flowing to the richer sectors of global society such that the underlying growth-motivated logic of capitalism was sustained?'

We argued empirically that, on the basis of this modelling, at the $2 and $4 poverty lines, there was enough growth 1990–2012 to share, in order to have ended poverty at those lines. Our primary finding is that a very modest amount of redistribution of the global consumption growth increment since 1990 could have ended $2 (2011 PPP) poverty already. In short, growth would not have to have been much more inclusive to end poverty at $2 already. Perhaps some additional fairly minor tax and transfers could have achieved it by now. One could label this as 'global philanthropy', since the small size of this redistribution would not really have had any fundamental impact on the contemporary model of capitalism.

This is not to say that achieving that redistribution would have been easy. Although the redistribution required would have been less than 1.5% of global consumption growth, this still amounts to an increase of around 70% in the share of growth that accrued to those currently on less than $2 a day. We argue that what this does illustrate, therefore, is that the problem of the persistence of $2 poverty should not be ascribed to insufficient consumption growth overall since 1990, and instead attention should be paid to the mechanisms and systems that account for the distribution of the growth that did take place.

There was more than enough growth to have removed $2 poverty through reallocation of the benefits of global growth from the global prosperiat (those consuming over $30 a day, a group that is just 10% of the world's population, but includes around half of the population of the HICs and accounts for almost half of global consumption) to the $2 poor without having any significant or, probably, even noticeable impact on the consumption levels of those richest 10% of the world's population.

However, $2 a day is an extremely low level of consumption. If one took a more reasonable poverty line, such as the median consumption of developing countries in 2012, of $4 per day, something more substantial is required. Ending poverty is still plausible. Indeed, ending $4 poverty could have been achieved while still allowing a substantial share of global consumption growth to accrue to the prosperiat. It would, though, have required a more substantial redistribution of growth: one that would imply some kind of significant welfare-oriented regimes around and towards the developing world, rather than just some minor additional tax and transfer or 'philanthropy'.

At higher poverty lines, such as the $10-a-day level at which the risk of falling back into poverty declines to a low probability, something much more radical would be required in terms of economic organisation. Welfare-oriented regimes would not be sufficient. Ending $10 poverty would require a reallocation, not only of *all* the prosperiat group's post-1990 consumption growth share, but also either a reduction of the prosperiat group's consumption to below 1990 standards, or a more extensive redistribution of the growth increment. This would effectively mean that per capita consumption levels of all those above $10 a day (not only the prosperiat on $30+ but also the securiat on $10–30) would have remained at or only slightly above their 1990 levels: a scenario that would imply a very radical shift in the forms of contemporary capitalism.

We therefore argue that the causes of the persistence of global absolute poverty, certainly at $2 and $4 per day, and its eventual elimination are less due to insufficient consumption growth overall than to the pattern of growth or the distribution of the growth increment which has not been conducive to eliminating poverty at $2 or $4. Eradicating $2 poverty may require some enhanced tax and transfers, but eradicating $4 poverty would require a substantial shift towards stronger global and national welfare regimes. This implies that a much greater focus in policy is needed on the governance of growth—managing the pattern of growth and who benefits—if $2 or $4 poverty are to be ended. And if $10 poverty is to be ended in coming decades, a radically new form of economic organisation is needed.

Our purpose here though is not to outline some sort of speculative or utopian transformation of the global economy. Our aim is actually much more pragmatic and immediate. The UN SDGs bring much more attention than did the MDGs on the quality and (in)equity of development. For example, the SDGs now address issues of inequality and inclusive growth as well as various aspects of poverty. This is laudable. However, the interconnections between some of these issues require greater attention. This is particularly the case when considering headline global poverty counts, where it is still unusual to consider, as we have done here, the wider implications (of allocation and distribution of growth) that are the corollaries inherent to the poverty lines adopted.

Instead, attention and effort are often directed to building 'precise' estimates of what the 'right' poverty line should be, based on assessments of consumption needs and living standards. For example, the World Bank has now adopted a range of poverty lines that it considers. The history of the World Bank's $1.90 extreme poverty line is instructive here. This line has been rebased from $1.00 a day in 1990 to $1.08 in 2001, $1.25 in 2008 and $1.90 in 2015. The rebasing has been occasioned by updates to PPP rates.

In each case, the methodology has also changed. Revisions have been based on different countries, different numbers of countries and different statistical approaches (mean or median, for example). At one level, this could be treated as trying to ensure consistency of at least headline numbers across different data sets, though changes in PPP rates do not only change headline poverty counts, they also change the geographical distribution of poverty. Efforts to align poverty lines from one PPP revision

6 CONCLUSION

to the next can therefore lead to the impression that there is much more consistency between the data sets than there actually is when one drills down into the details.

Our concerns here are reinforced when we consider the large inherent uncertainties in the processes by which the PPP rates are developed, and how these vary from one PPP data collection round to the next. In view of these processes, extended debates over whether a poverty line should be $1.90 or $2.00 or $2.10 look like an attempt to impose the impression of a precision onto data sets that are simply not robust enough to support such a precision. As we have shown, just a 10 cent difference in the choice of poverty line can make a difference of around 100 million to the global poverty count.

Rather than focusing on developing ever more 'precise' poverty line valuations, this hypersensitivity should alert us to the dangers of focusing on what the 'right' value for a global poverty line is, at the expense of asking what the different challenges of eradicating poverty would be if the sensitivities and uncertainties in the data were properly recognised and their implications more broadly considered, as we do here. (Incidentally, this is also the reason why we have chosen here to use poverty lines rounded to the nearest whole dollar rather than to use the World Bank poverty lines.)

There is an extensive literature on what precisely the 'right' consumption poverty line should be. In contrast, relatively little has been written on the political consequences in distribution terms that are inherent to different poverty lines. Thus, we would argue that attempts to improve the accuracy of the measurement of poverty may be a distraction. In short, the search for ever more precision in global poverty measurement diverts attention away from the more difficult nature and extent of the political challenges that are inherent to different poverty lines.

What we have really been trying to do in this book, therefore, is draw attention to how the way one approaches global data on poverty and inequality—that is, the questions one asks of the data, the degree to which one explores the data in its entirety, and the extent to which one works with and within the limitations of the data—has a very significant impact on the narratives that one develops from the data. And narratives are political, in the sense that they have effects in shaping how we make sense of the world, and therefore how we understand where we stand in the world, and where we stand in relation to what we think needs to change in the world.

This book has sought to show that there are alternative ways of thinking, or narratives, about the challenge of eradicating global poverty. At this moment in time, this is particularly important because the biggest difference between the MDGs and the current SDGs is that a lot more issues related to inclusion and inequality are present in the SDGs. If the SDGs' aspiration to end global poverty 'in all its forms' is to be achieved, then more questions need to be asked about the concomitant political implications. Our hope is that in some small way, this book can contribute to a growing recognition of the importance of raising such questions.

CHAPTER 7

Methodological Annex

Abstract In this annex, we discuss in further depth the methodology used in the GrIP model.

Keywords Poverty · Inequality · Growth

This book makes use of a custom-built model of growth, inequality and poverty. Henceforth, this model is referred to as the GrIP ('Gr'owth, 'I'nequality and 'P'overty) model (version 2.0, 2015). For an earlier version of the model (GrIP model v1.0), see Edward and Sumner (2014). The GrIP model includes extensive functionality to test the sensitivity of results to different data sets, and different assumptions about how to handle the data. The descriptions provided in this book relate only to the model as configured for the analysis presented here, and should not be assumed to apply to the way the model is configured in other published analyses based on the GrIP model.

For this book, we have configured GrIP to align with the overall approach used by the World Bank when producing poverty estimates through PovcalNet. This means that our approach here is to combine survey distributions with survey (rather than NA) means, and to rely wherever possible on data in Povcal in preference to other sources, on the basis that data in Povcal has already been selected for reliability and robustness through scrutiny of available competing survey data sets.

This does not mean that GrIP replicates Povcal calculations, because there are a number of additional adjustments in GrIP that are included to develop a truly global distribution that can allow reasonable comparison across time periods. Principal among these are: the use of other sources and methods to add in estimates for countries where data is not available in Povcal; the way that underlying survey data is interpolated between surveys; and the use of changes in NA data to inform scaling of survey means (mean per capita consumption) between surveys. We describe these adjustments briefly below, but because they were originally introduced in earlier versions of GrIP after careful consideration and evaluation, we would refer the reader to earlier discussions of the GrIP (e.g. Edward and Sumner 2013a, b, 2014) and later papers too where much more detail can be found (e.g. Edward and Sumner 2015a, b, 2016, 2018).

In this book, we also introduce two new additional measures, namely the adjustment of income-based surveys to align more consistently with consumption-based surveys, and an adjustment to estimate the possible impact of top income earners who are often missed from surveys. These are new adjustments; thus, we discuss them in more detail.

The core approach in the GrIP model is to take for each country the distribution (quintile and decile) data and, by combining this with data on national population and on the mean consumption per capita in internationally comparable PPP $, develop for each country an estimate of how many people live at any specific consumption ($-a-day) level. Having identified for each country the number of people living at each consumption level, the GrIP model then aggregates these to build a global distribution of how many people live, and how much those people consume, at every consumption level, from the poorest to the richest in the world, and a wide variety of sub-global aggregations are also readily produced. These aggregations are then interrogated to investigate issues such as poverty levels, trends in inequality, and who are the absolute or relative winners and losers from global growth.

The GrIP v2.0 is built from data in the World Bank's PovcalNet, World Development Indicators, UNU-WIDER's WIID3b and UN Population Division World Population Prospects.

Throughout this book, we use the new PPP rates (for 2011). While we acknowledge that significant uncertainties remain concerning this data (for a discussion of these issues see Edward and Sumner 2015a), nevertheless we use them because we recognise that they are generally thought to be the best available data and superior to previous PPP data (Deaton and Aten 2014).

Distributions (quintile and upper and lower decile data) are taken (in this order of preference) from PovcalNet, World Development Indicators or the UNU WIID database. Survey data has improved considerably in recent years and, notably, there are now many more surveys to draw data from and far fewer 'gaps' for specific countries. However, there are still some significant gaps in the data. Surveys do not take place annually so, in the GrIP model, distributions for intermediate years between surveys are calculated by interpolation, while in years subsequent to the most recent survey, the distribution is assumed to remain unchanged from that survey.

We note also that the distribution data can be derived at either the individual level or the household level. This is an outcome of the original survey design and so it is difficult to adjust for in subsequent analysis. As is the case for most other studies, we do not attempt to adjust for this difference but note that household surveys will inevitably understate national inequality to some extent as they do not include intra-household inequality. To ensure optimum coverage of the global population, where a country has no surveys, or the gaps between surveys are too great to allow reliable interpolation, the GrIP model 'fills' a country's missing distributions with the (not population-weighted) average distribution from all other countries in the same region and income group (in contrast, the World Bank poverty estimates are based on 'filling' with regional averages regardless of average income; see, for details, Ferreira et al. 2015).

The GrIP v2.0 model (as configured here) calculates the number of people in each country at each different consumption level by combining survey distributions with measures of mean per capita consumption. The model then disaggregates these national populations into globally standard '$ per capita' brackets, thereby avoiding introducing the distortions of approaches, such as Bhalla's simple accounting procedure (Bhalla 2002; Hillebrand 2008) where, by disaggregating to percentiles, some large step-change distortions are introduced in the later global aggregation at points where percentiles from the very largest countries (such as India and China where each percentile currently includes well over 10 million people) are added back into the global distribution.

In earlier versions of the GrIP model, a linear distribution algorithm was used that accurately replicates the consumption level in each fractile in the source data. This works well in the lower fractiles where poverty headcounts are estimated, but at the higher end of the distribution (typically the upper quintile: the highest consuming 20%), while it accurately reproduces the totals of these top two deciles, it does so at the expense of significant oversimplification of the large variations in inequality within those deciles. In the GrIP v2.0 model, the generalised quadratic (GQ) algorithm, as described by Datt (1998), has also been incorporated. Arguably, this algorithm can replicate better the inequality distribution within the highest deciles so, in this book, we use the GQ algorithm throughout.

Changes in consumption mean between survey years are derived by combining year-on-year changes in Household Final Consumption Expenditure (HFCE) from national account (NA) data with changes in the country-specific ratio of HFCE per capita means and survey-based means (the NA/S ratio) in survey years. We have previously used GrIP to explore the impact of different approaches and assumptions in the use of the available data. For example, Edward and Sumner (2014) compare NA and survey means with reference to global and regional poverty estimates and discuss how the use of NA means makes a substantial difference to estimates of global poverty and global inequality. Edward and Sumner (2015a, b) compare 2005 and 2011 PPPs. We do this here to remain comparable to the reference literature (such as poverty estimates published by the World Bank). Where reliable survey means are not available (for example, when filling countries for which there is no survey data, or when using distributions from WDI where survey means are not provided), an appropriate survey mean is estimated for that country based on its average per capita consumption level. To do this, we use the following relationship, derived from the consumption surveys in PovcalNet:

$$\left(\frac{NA}{S}\right)_{consumption} = (\text{HFCE per capita})^\alpha$$

The question of how NA means correlate with survey means has long been considered problematic (see, for example, Altimir 1987; Mejía and Vos 1997; Ravallion 2003; Deaton 2001). Karshenas (2003) identifies that a systemic relationship appears to exist between NA and survey means, but that this is subject to considerable variation between countries. For this reason, in GrIP we use country-specific NA/S ratios wherever possible and include estimates generalised from global data only where necessary. A fuller description of our approach has been provided elsewhere (Edward 2006; Edward and Sumner 2013a, b, 2014) although recent increases in available data mean that in GrIP v2.0, we have improved the method of estimation by introducing the regression relationship described here. We estimate that $\alpha = 0.052$.

GrIP v2.0 incorporates two important developments compared to v1.0. These are: the introduction of an adjustment of income-based surveys to render them more comparable to consumption-based surveys; and an adjustment to estimate the effect of top income earners who are often missed from national consumption or income surveys.

It is widely recognised that there is likely to be a systematic difference between measures of consumption distribution and those of income distribution. In World Bank calculations where there has been the option of choosing either an income or consumption-based set of measures (i.e. distribution data and matching mean), there has been a preference for using consumption-based measures. While an argument can be made that this is because poverty lines are nominally translatable into actual consumption (of food, shelter, etc.) and so consumption levels are a better reflection of an individual's welfare, the more compelling explanation is generally that, among those at the bottom of the distribution, measures of income can be less reliable due to underreporting or misrecognition of informal incomes or the value of self-produced incomes (such as directly consumed agricultural produce). For these sorts of reasons, World Bank estimates have tended to prefer using consumption measures (see discussion of Lipton and Ravallion 1995) and in the spirit of mirroring (but not directly replicating) the Povcal approach, we do likewise here.

Until recently, however, most analyses of global poverty and inequality (including, but not only, earlier versions of the GrIP model) have not made any adjustment for systemic differences between consumption-based and income-based measures, opting instead merely to use consumption-based measures whenever a direct choice is available. A key pragmatic reason as to why this adjustment has been often omitted is because within PovcalNet, there is only a rather limited set of countries where equivalent data (i.e. from the same country and same year) is provided on both an income and a consumption basis, and from which therefore a suitable comparison and adjustment could be developed. This comparison has now become more feasible with the latest updates of PovcalNet and WIID, which contain a much larger number of paired income and consumption surveys, and so we are now able to introduce this adjustment.

The paper of Deininger and Squire (1996) was one of the first to estimate adjustments for consumption to income measures. Niño-Zarazúa et al. (2014, p. 11) suggest adding 7.8 points to the consumption Gini, though 6.6 lies within the 95% confidence interval of their estimate. More recently, and using the latest WIID, Lahoti et al. (2014) identify 120 instances in the WIID data set where there are both consumption and income distributions reported by the same statistical agency in the same year for a country. From these, they estimate conversion factors to transform quintile data based on income metrics to consumption-equivalent values. We have not repeated their calculations; instead, we have used the more limited set of PovcalNet data to develop comparable estimates. In Table 7.1, estimate 'a' is derived from pairs of income and consumption surveys made in the same year. Estimate 'b' pairs income surveys with consumption surveys made within one year of each other.

Despite using a much more limited data set, these estimates broadly confirm figures from Lahoti et al. (2014) and demonstrate that (as one would expect) consumption distributions are less unequal with a higher proportion of the distribution accruing to the lower fractiles.

Table 7.1 Conversion multipliers for adjusting income survey data

	Estimate 'a' Source: PovcalNet	Estimate 'b' Source: PovcalNet	Estimate 'c' Source: Lahoti et al. (2014)
No. of matched surveys in sample	25	39	120
No. of countries in sample	8	15	Not stated
Decile 1 (D1)	1.399	1.598	1.386*
Quintile 1 (Q1)	1.196	1.318	1.185
Quintile 2 (Q2)	1.045	1.091	1.150
Quintile 3 (Q3)	1.030	1.048	1.120
Quintile 4 (Q4)	1.014	1.011	1.060
Quintile 5 (Q5)	0.966	0.936	0.860
Decile 10 (D10)	0.955	0.919	0.851*

Note *Data estimated by authors
Source Authors' estimates based on GrIP v2.0 and Lahoti et al. (2014)

In this book, we have adopted the Lahoti et al. adjustments (because they are derived from a much larger data set) and supplemented them by our own estimate (derived from estimates 'a' and 'b') for the lowest and highest deciles, as these are not stated by Lahoti et al. We would note, however, that a substantial degree of uncertainty remains over this relationship (see discussion in Atkinson and Brandolini 2001).

Applying these multipliers to a country's decile/quintile figures (if the original data is based on income measures) adjusts the income-based distributions in the model to make them more comparable to consumption-based measures. However, these systemic differences are not limited to the distribution curves. There is also a systematic difference between income-based means and consumption-based means, with income measured in the surveys being on average larger than consumption measured in the surveys (see, for example, Karshenas 2003, p. 691), so that an adjustment also needs to be made to reduce the income aggregate (or mean) to render it comparable to consumption aggregates. We address this by revisiting the calculation of the NA/S to HFCE relationship (discussed above), but this time we use only income surveys (whereas previously it was calculated using only consumption surveys). This allows us to use all the surveys in PovcalNet (of which over 500 are income based and over 600 are consumption based, as opposed to the much more limited set of fewer than 40 paired income and consumption surveys) to estimate a relationship between consumption and income-based NA/S ratios as follows (we estimate that $\beta = -0.024$):

$$\left(\frac{NA}{S}\right)_{consumption} = \left(\frac{NA}{S}\right)_{income} \times (HFCE\ per\ capita)^{\beta}$$

All results presented in this book include this adjustment of income surveys to consumption equivalents. Although intuitively one would expect income-based means to be larger than consumption-based means, the reasons are complex and are different depending, for example, on where an individual is on the distribution. For further discussion, see Deaton (2005) who analyses the issue in detail and Altimir (1987) who discusses some of the complexity inherent to different approaches to income surveys, and the difficulties encountered in trying to disaggregate and account for individual elements of this complexity. For these reasons, here we follow Lahoti et al. (2014) in deriving generalised adjustment factors from the aggregated data that can be applied to bring income-based measures more closely into alignment with consumption-based measures than has been standard practice in the past.

It has long been recognised that the consumption (or income) of the top of the distribution is not well captured in the household survey data (see, for discussion, Korinek et al. 2006). More recently, data from the Paris School of Economics' *Top Incomes Project* (TIP) (which is based on taxation data; see Alvaredo et al. 2014) has drawn attention to concerns that the 'missing' share of the distribution that accrues to the top percentiles can be substantial. Various methods have been proposed recently to take account of this. Some scholars have attempted to adjust for 'top incomes' by assuming that discrepancies between survey and HFCE data are entirely due to underreporting by the richest (e.g. Lakner and Milanovic 2013). Others (e.g. Anand and Segal 2015) develop assumptions on the missing 'top incomes' by drawing on the TIP data produced by Alvaredo et al. (2014).

More commonly, the issue has been expediently ignored on the basis that if one is only concerned with estimating poverty levels then the problem of 'missing' consumption of the richest is largely incidental because it occurs at the top of the country distributions, and so generally well above the poverty lines under consideration.

However, the issue could make a difference when considering the entire global consumption distribution, as we do here, so in the GrIP v2.0 model we use the TIP data set to develop a relationship between the share of the top decile (10%) from national distribution surveys and the reported shares in TIP (from tax data) of the top fractiles, i.e. the top decile (10%), ventile (5%) and percentile (1%). We use the most recent surveys from each country in TIP where there is both a matching income-based survey in PovcalNet and data in TIP. This yields 17 datapoints (all of which are from HICs), from which we derive linear relationships to estimate the unadjusted top decile share in the survey distributions in GrIP, and revised shares of the top decile, ventile and percentile in each country. The data in GrIP is then adjusted by adding consumption appropriately across the top decile in every country, to bring the shares of the top fractiles in line with these estimated revised shares. Recognising, however, that the HFCE figure probably provides an upper limit to the amount of consumption that should reasonably be added, we cap the adjustment so that the total consumption for each country does not exceed its HFCE total. There are some exceptions to this where the PovcalNet survey mean already implies a consumption

7 METHODOLOGICAL ANNEX

Table 7.2 Estimates of scale of redistribution of the growth increment, 1990–2012 to eradicate $2 poverty, *with* top income adjustment

	Amount available for within-country and global transfers ($bn)	No. of countries that can afford to remove poverty without global transfers	No. of countries that require global transfers	Total poverty headcount (millions)	Poverty headcount in countries that can afford to remove poverty without global transfers (millions)	Amount transferred within-country ($bn)	Poverty gap remaining after within-country transfers ($bn)	Total available for global transfers ($bn)	Amount received in global transfer ($bn)	Amount provided to global transfer ($bn)	Total amount transferred (within-country and global) ($bn)	Cover ratio (%, all transfers)
Total	3136.4	48	57	935	493	93.0	100.1	3043.4	100.1	100.1	193.1	6.2
China	518.8	1	0	84	84	11.3	0.0	507.5	0.0	16.7	28.0	5.4
India	78.3	1	0	292	292	42.8	0.0	35.6	0.0	1.2	43.9	56.1
East Asia and Pacific	1105.9	12	6	131	127	15.9	0.9	1090.0	0.9	35.8	51.7	4.7
Europe and Central Asia	776.8	4	7	11	1	0.2	2.3	776.7	2.3	25.5	25.7	3.3
Latin America and Caribbean	120.5	21	7	54	36	8.0	3.9	112.5	3.9	3.7	11.7	9.7
Middle East and North Africa	44.3	0	3	3	0	0.0	0.3	44.3	0.3	1.5	1.5	3.3

(continued)

Table 7.2 (continued)

	Amount available for within-country and global transfers ($bn)	No. of countries that can afford to remove poverty without global transfers	No. of countries that require global transfers	Total poverty headcount (millions)	Poverty headcount in countries that can afford to remove poverty without global transfers (millions)	Amount transferred within-country ($bn)	Poverty gap remaining after within-country transfers ($bn)	Total available for global transfers ($bn)	Amount received in global transfer ($bn)	Amount provided to global transfer ($bn)	Total amount transferred (within-country and global) ($bn)	Cover ratio (%, all transfers)
North America	937.0	0	0	0	0	0.0	0.0	937.0	0.0	30.8	30.8	3.3
South Asia Region	105.5	2	1	351	295	49.0	3.7	56.6	3.7	1.9	50.8	48.2
Sub-Saharan Africa	46.4	9	33	385	34	20.0	88.9	26.4	88.9	0.9	20.9	45.0
E. Asia less China	587.1	11	6	47	43	4.6	0.9	582.5	0.9	19.2	23.8	4.0
S. Asia less India	27.2	1	1	59	3	6.2	3.7	21.0	3.7	0.7	6.9	25.3
High—OECD	1817.9	2	0	1	1	0.1	0.0	1817.8	0.0	59.8	59.9	3.3
High—non-OECD	283.9	8	0	0	0	0.0	0.0	283.9	0.0	9.3	9.4	3.3
LIC and MIC	1034.6	38	57	934	492	92.9	100.1	941.7	100.1	31.0	123.8	12.0

(continued)

Table 7.2 (continued)

	Amount available for within-country and global transfers ($bn)	No. of countries that can afford to remove poverty without global transfers	No. of countries that require global transfers	Total poverty headcount (millions)	Poverty headcount in countries that can afford to remove poverty without global transfers (millions)	Amount transferred within-country ($bn)	Poverty gap remaining after within-country transfers ($bn)	Total available for global transfers ($bn)	Amount received in global transfer ($bn)	Amount provided to global transfer ($bn)	Total amount transferred (within-country and global) ($bn)	Cover ratio (%, all transfers)
UMIC	742.3	20	10	146	125	19.0	5.2	723.3	5.2	23.8	42.8	5.8
LMIC	273.8	15	23	457	345	58.4	19.2	215.4	19.2	7.1	65.5	23.9
UMIC (excl. China)	223.5	19	10	62	40	7.7	5.2	215.8	5.2	7.1	14.8	6.6
LMIC (excl. India)	195.4	14	23	166	54	15.6	19.2	179.8	19.2	5.9	21.5	11.0
LIC	18.5	3	24	331	22	15.4	75.6	3.1	75.6	0.1	15.5	84.0
LDCs	20.1	6	32	342	24	15.8	78.0	4.4	78.0	0.1	15.9	79.0
Fragile states	3.6	2	19	128	3	2.9	39.4	0.7	39.4	0.0	2.9	81.9

Source GrIP v2.0

Table 7.3 Estimates of scale of redistribution of the growth increment, 1990–2012 to eradicate $4 poverty, *with* top income adjustment

	Amount available for within-country and global transfers ($bn)	No. of countries that can afford to remove poverty without global transfers	No. of countries that require global transfers	Total poverty headcount (millions)	Poverty headcount in countries that can afford to remove poverty without global transfers (millions)	Amount transferred within-country ($bn)	Poverty gap remaining after within-country transfers ($bn)	Total available for global transfers ($bn)	Amount received in global transfer ($bn)	Amount provided to global transfer ($bn)	Total amount transferred (within-country and global) ($bn)	Cover ratio (%, all transfers)
Total	3136.4	55	83	2606	612	433.8	1091.5	2702.6	1091.5	1091.5	1525.3	48.6
China	518.8	1	0	360	360	166.9	0.0	351.9	0.0	142.1	309.0	59.6
India	78.3	0	1	907	0	78.3	430.0	0.0	430.0	0.0	78.3	100.0
East Asia and Pacific	1105.9	13	10	567	507	244.8	21.4	861.1	21.4	347.8	592.6	53.6
Europe and Central Asia	776.8	14	9	44	12	4.0	17.5	772.8	17.5	312.1	316.1	40.7
Latin America and Caribbean	120.5	17	15	157	48	44.9	44.4	75.6	44.4	30.5	75.4	62.6
Middle East and North Africa	44.3	4	5	50	14	3.5	13.5	40.8	13.5	16.5	20.0	45.1
North America	937.0	1	0	4	4	0.7	0.0	936.3	0.0	378.1	378.9	40.4
South Asia Region	105.5	2	4	1124	4	96.7	525.7	8.8	525.7	3.6	100.3	95.0
Sub-Saharan Africa	46.4	4	40	661	23	39.2	469.0	7.2	469.0	2.9	42.1	90.7

(continued)

Table 7.3 (continued)

	Amount available for within-country and global transfers ($bn)	No. of countries that can afford to remove poverty without global transfers	No. of countries that require global transfers	Total poverty headcount (millions)	Poverty headcount in countries that can afford to remove poverty without global transfers (millions)	Amount transferred within-country ($bn)	Poverty gap remaining after within-country transfers ($bn)	Total available for global transfers ($bn)	Amount received in global transfer ($bn)	Amount provided to global transfer ($bn)	Total amount transferred (within-country and global) ($bn)	Cover ratio (%, all transfers)
E. Asia less China	587.1	12	10	207	147	77.9	21.4	509.2	21.4	205.7	283.6	48.3
S. Asia less India	27.2	2	3	217	4	18.4	95.7	8.8	95.7	3.6	21.9	80.7
High-OECD	1817.9	10	1	13	10	2.7	0.8	1815.3	0.8	733.1	735.8	40.5
High-non-OECD	283.9	13	1	2	2	0.8	0.0	283.1	0.0	114.3	115.2	40.6
LIC and MIC	1034.6	32	81	2592	600	430.3	1090.7	604.3	1090.7	244.1	674.3	65.2
UMIC	742.3	21	21	563	440	224.3	51.0	518.1	51.0	209.2	433.5	58.4
LMIC	273.8	11	33	1467	160	187.5	623.1	86.2	623.1	34.8	222.3	81.2
UMIC (excl. China)	223.5	20	21	203	81	57.3	51.0	166.2	51.0	67.1	124.5	55.7
LMIC (excl. India)	195.4	11	32	560	160	109.2	193.1	86.2	193.1	34.8	144.0	73.7
LIC	18.5	0	27	562	0	18.5	416.6	0.0	416.6	0.0	18.5	100.0
LDCs	20.1	2	37	596	0	19.3	435.1	0.8	435.1	0.3	19.7	97.7
Fragile states	3.6	0	21	200	0	3.6	162.4	0.0	162.4	0.0	3.6	100.0

Source GrIP v2.0

Table 7.4 Estimates of scale of redistribution of the growth increment, 1990–2012 to eradicate $10 poverty, *with* top income adjustment

	Amount available for with-in-country and global transfers ($bn)	No. of countries that can afford to remove poverty without global transfers	No. of countries that require global transfers	Total poverty head-count (millions)	Poverty headcount in countries that can afford to remove poverty without global transfers (millions)	Amount transferred with-in-country ($bn)	Poverty gap remaining after with-in-country transfers ($bn)	Total available for global transfers ($bn)	Amount received in global transfer ($bn)	Amount provided to global transfer ($bn)	Total amount transferred (with-in-country and global) ($bn)	Cover ratio (%, all transfers)
Total	3136.4	44	125	4514	156	1141.4	8611.7	1995.1	1995.1	1995.1	3136.4	100.0
China	518.8	0	1	936	0	518.8	1164.1	0.0	269.7	0.0	518.8	100.0
India	78.3	0	1	1147	0	78.3	2810.5	0.0	651.1	0.0	78.3	100.0
East Asia and Pacific	1105.9	7	19	1387	20	694.2	1862.6	411.6	431.5	411.6	1105.9	100.0
Europe and Central Asia	776.8	27	16	208	93	114.6	167.3	662.2	38.8	662.2	776.8	100.0
Latin America and Caribbean	120.5	4	28	367	3	117.1	570.8	3.4	132.2	3.4	120.5	100.0
Middle East and North Africa	44.3	3	12	208	3	19.5	295.6	24.9	68.5	24.9	44.3	100.0
North America	937.0	3	0	37	37	44.1	0.0	892.9	0.0	892.9	937.0	100.0
South Asia Region	105.5	0	6	1497	0	105.5	3577.7	0.0	828.9	0.0	105.5	100.0
Sub-Saharan Africa	46.4	0	44	810	0	46.4	2137.6	0.0	495.2	0.0	46.4	100.0

(continued)

Table 7.4 (continued)

	Amount available for with-in-country and global transfers ($bn)	No. of countries that can afford to remove poverty without global transfers	No. of countries that require global transfers	Total poverty head-count (millions)	Poverty headcount in countries that can afford to remove poverty without global transfers (millions)	Amount transferred with-in-country ($bn)	Poverty gap remaining after with-in-country transfers ($bn)	Total available for global transfers ($bn)	Amount received in global transfer ($bn)	Amount provided to global transfer ($bn)	Total amount transferred (with-in-country and global) ($bn)	Cover ratio (%, all transfers)
E. Asia less China	587.1	7	18	451	20	175.5	698.5	411.6	161.8	411.6	587.1	100.0
S. Asia less India	27.2	0	5	350	0	27.2	767.3	0.0	177.8	0.0	27.2	100.0
High—OECD	1817.9	26	3	116	99	113.9	15.9	1704.0	3.7	1704.0	1817.9	100.0
High—non-OECD	283.9	11	10	42	34	35.1	6.2	248.9	1.4	248.9	283.9	100.0
LIC and MIC	1034.6	7	112	4355	24	992.4	8589.6	42.2	1990.0	42.2	1034.6	100.0
UMIC	742.3	6	41	1502	14	718.3	1944.7	24.1	450.5	24.1	742.3	100.0
LMIC	273.8	1	44	2207	10	255.6	4873.2	18.1	1129.0	18.1	273.8	100.0
UMIC (excl. China)	223.5	6	40	566	14	199.5	780.6	24.1	180.8	24.1	223.5	100.0
LMIC (excl. India)	195.4	1	43	1060	10	177.3	2062.7	18.1	477.9	18.1	195.4	100.0
LIC	18.5	0	27	646	0	18.5	1771.7	0.0	410.5	0.0	18.5	100.0
LDCs	20.1	0	39	701	0	20.1	1897.7	0.0	439.7	0.0	20.1	100.0
Fragile states	3.6	0	21	250	0	3.6	678.2	0.0	157.1	0.0	3.6	100.0

Source GrIP v2.0

level higher than the HFCE total. In those cases, we reason that the HFCE figures must be questionable and so do not apply the cap.

This adjustment does not have any impact on the absolute consumption of those below the top decile in each country. It simply adds consumption to the top 10% in each country and distributes this so as to reproduce, in GrIP's consumption-based analysis, the same share of the distribution that the TIP database identifies for and among the top 10%. In practice, however, the share of the rich in a consumption survey will probably be lower than this, as rich people tend to save more and consume less, as a proportion of their annual income, than do the poor. For these reasons, we consider that the top incomes adjustment in GrIP may overstate the share of consumption that is accounted for by the richest decile in each country. We therefore present estimates with and without top income adjustment on the basis that such estimates might be best viewed as bracketing a high and low scenario that cover the range of possibilities, not that one or the other is more 'correct' (Tables 7.2, 7.3, and 7.4).

REFERENCES

Altimir, O. (1987). Income distribution statistics in Latin America and their reliability. *Review of Income and Wealth, 33*(2), 111–155.

Alvaredo, F., Atkinson, A., Piketty, T., & Saez, E. (2014). *The world top incomes database*. http://wid.world.

Anand, S., & Segal, P. (2015). The global distribution of income. In Anthony B. Atkinson & François Bourguignon (Eds.), *Handbook of income distribution* (Vol. 2). Amsterdam: Elsevier.

Atkinson, A. B., & Brandolini, A. (2001). Promise and pitfalls in the use of 'secondary' data-sets: Income inequality in OECD countries as a case study. *Journal of Economic Literature, 39*(3), 771–799.

Bhalla, S. (2002). *Imagine there's no country: Poverty, inequality and growth in the era of globalization*. Washington, DC: Institute for International Economics.

Datt, G. (1998). *Computational tools for poverty measurement and analysis* (FCND Discussion Papers). Washington, DC: International Food Policy Research Institute (IFPRI).

Deaton, A. (2001). Counting the world's poor: Problems and possible solutions. *The World Bank Research Observer, 16*(2), 125–147.

Deaton, A. (2005). Measuring poverty in a growing world (or measuring growth in a poor world). *The Review of Economics and Statistics, 87*(1), 1–19.

Deaton, A., & Aten, B. (2014). *Trying to understand the PPPs in ICP2011: Why are the results so different?* (National Bureau of Economic Research Working Paper 20244). Cambridge, MA: NBER.

Deininger, K., & Squire, L. (1996). A new data set measuring income inequality. *World Bank Economic Review, 10,* 565–591.

Edward, P. (2006). Examining inequality: Who really benefits from global growth? *World Development, 34*(10), 1667–1695.

Edward, P., & Sumner, A. (2013a). *The future of global poverty in a multi-speed world: New estimates of scale and location, 2010–2030* (Center for Global Development Working Paper 327). Washington, DC: CGD.

Edward, P., & Sumner, A. (2013b). *The geography of inequality: Where and by how much has income distribution changed since 1990?* (Centre for Global Development Working Paper 341). Washington, DC: CGD.

Edward, P., & Sumner, A. (2014). Estimating the scale and geography of global poverty now and in the future: How much difference do method and assumptions make? *World Development, 58,* 67–82.

Edward, P., & Sumner, A. (2015a). *New estimates of global poverty and inequality: How much difference do price data really make?* (Center for Global Development Working Paper 403). Washington, DC: CGD.

Edward, P., & Sumner, A. (2015b). Philanthropy, welfare capitalism or radically different global economic model: What would it take to end global poverty within a generation based on historical growth patterns? (Center for Global Development [CGD] Working Paper). Washington DC: CGD.

Edward, P., & Sumner, A. (2016). *Global inequality and global poverty since the Cold War?* (CROP Working Paper). Bergen: CROP/UiB.

Edward, P., & Sumner, A. (2018). Global poverty and inequality: Are the revised estimates open to an alternative interpretation? *Third World Quarterly, 39*(3), 487–509.

Ferreira, F., Chen, S., & Dabalen, A. L., et al. (2015). *A global count of the extreme poor in 2012: Data issues, methodology, and initial results* (World Bank Working Paper). Washington, DC: World Bank.

Hillebrand, E. (2008). The global distribution of income in 2050. *World Development, 36*(5), 727–740.

Karshenas, M. (2003). Global poverty: National accounts based versus survey based estimates. *Development and Change, 34*(4), 683–712.

Korinek, A., Mistiaen, J., & Ravallion, M. (2006). Survey nonresponse and the distribution of income. *Journal of Economic Inequality, 4*(2), 33–55.

Lahoti, R., Jayadev, A., & Reddy, S. (2014). *The global consumption and income project (GCIP): An introduction and preliminary findings.* www.globalconsumptionandincomeproject.org. Accessed 4 June 2018.

Lakner, C., & Milanovic, B. (2013). *Global income distribution: From the fall of the Berlin wall to the great recession* (World Bank Policy Research Working Paper 6719). Washington, DC: World Bank.

Lipton, M., & Ravallion, M. (1995). Poverty and policy. In J. Behrman & T. N. Srinivasan (Eds.), *Handbook of development economics* (Vol. 3a). Amsterdam: North-Holland.

Mejía, J. A., & Vos, R. (1997). *Poverty in Latin America and the Caribbean: An inventory: 1980–95*. Washington, DC: Inter-American Development Bank.

Niño-Zarazúa, M., Roope, L., & Tarp, F. (2014). *Global interpersonal inequality: Trends and measurement* (WIDER Working Paper 2014/004). Helsinki: WIDER.

Ravallion, M. (2003). Measuring aggregate welfare in developing countries: How well do national accounts and surveys agree? *The Review of Economics and Statistics, 85*(3), 645–652.

Index

A
Absolute poor, 25, 26, 28
Adams, R., 5
Allen, R., 24, 40
Altimir, O., 72, 75
Alvaredo, F., 15
Anand, S., 15
Anderson, E., 6
Aten, B., 12, 71
Atkinson, A., 15

B
Berg, A., 8
Bhalla, S., 71
Birdsall, N., 24
Bluhm, R., 6
Bourguignon, F., 5
Brandolini, A., 75

C
Capitalism
 philanthropy, 48
 radical new model of, 60
 welfare, 60
Chen, A.L., 6

D
Dabalen, 6
Dang, H-A., 13
Datt, G., 15, 72
Deaton, A., 12, 14, 23, 71, 72, 75
De Crombrugghe, D., 6
Deininger, K., 74
Dercon, S., 6
Destitute, 25, 26, 30, 31, 45, 46–48, 60
Dollar, D., 6
Dollar-a-day
 $2 per day, 5, 6, 24, 25, 33, 38, 39, 63, 65, 66
 $4 per day, 38, 65, 66
 $10 per day, 18, 28
 and poverty headcount and gap, 22
 and PPP revisions, 66
 contentions, 39

ending of global poverty, 63
estimates, 12
limitations, 28, 29
national, 12, 70
PPP (purchasing power parity) data, 6
sensitivity of global poverty numbers, 23
surveys, 12

E
Easterly, W., 8, 24
Economic growth
and poverty, 42
distribution of, 12
inclusivity, 66
poverty efficiency of, 7
rate of, 50

F
Ferreira, F., 6, 23
Fosu, A., 6

G
Global consumption density curves, 28, 29
Global growth incidence curves, 29, 32, 33
Global inequality
estimates, 72
measures of, 71
Global population density curves, 17, 18
Global poverty
end of, 1, 2, 45
estimates, 2
gap, 38, 41, 42
lines, 24
sensitivity of global poverty to poverty lines, 22
GrIP (Growth, Inequality and Poverty) model
adjustment, 11, 13, 15, 18, 70, 73, 84
construction, 11
data sets, 11, 16, 69, 76
PPPs, 12–14

H
Hillebrand, E., 6, 71

J
Jayadev, A., 13, 74
Jolliffe, D., 23, 25, 27

K
Kalwij, A., 6
Karshenas, M., 72, 75
Karver, J., 6
Kenny, C., 6
Kharas, H., 24
Kleineberg, T., 6
Korinek, A., 15, 76
Kraay, A., 6

L
Lahoti, R., 13, 23, 74
Lakner, C., 15, 76
Lanjouw, P., 13
Lea, N., 6
Linder, S.B., 24
Lipton, M., 73
Loayza, N., 6
López-Calva, Luis F., 28
Luebker, M., 8
Lustig, N., 24

INDEX

M
Mejía, J.A., 72
Meyer, C., 24
Milanovic, B., 15, 76
Mistiaen, J., 15, 76

N
Niño-Zarazúa, M., 74

O
Ortiz-Juarez, E., 28
Ostry, J., 8

P
Perotti, R., 8
Piketty, T., 15
Pogge, T., 23
Precariat, 25, 26–28, 30, 31, 33, 34, 39, 46, 47, 60
Prosperiat, 25, 26, 27, 29, 30, 31, 33, 35, 36, 46–50, 58–61, 65
Prydz, E., 23, 25, 27

Q
Quah, D., 18

R
Raddatz, C., 6
Ravallion, M., 6, 14, 15, 23, 24, 72, 73, 76
Rebelo, S., 8
Reddy, S., 13, 23, 74
Redistribution
and poverty, 45, 49, 58
of the growth increment, 8, 45, 48, 50, 51, 53, 56, 65, 77, 80, 82
Roope, L., 74

S
Saez, E., 15
Sala-i-Martin, X., 14
Sanchez, C., 23
Securiat, 25, 26, 28, 30, 33, 34, 46, 49, 59–61, 65
Segal, P., 15
Serajuddin, U., 13
Squire, L., 74
Standing, G., 28
Szirmai, A., 6

T
Tarp, F., 74
Top incomes
adjustment, 16, 17, 27, 29, 30, 32–35, 46, 49, 51, 53, 56, 60, 61, 77, 80, 82, 84
data, 15, 16, 33, 60, 61, 76
Tsangarides, C., 8

V
Verschoor, A., 6
Vos, R., 72

W
White, H., 6
World Bank
global poverty estimates, 14, 71
poverty lines, 67
World Development Indicators, 70

Printed by Printforce, the Netherlands